Conference on Empirical Methods in Natural Language Processing (EMNLP 2023)

AA005151

Tutorial Abstracts

Singapore
6 - 10 December 2023

ISBN: 978-1-7138-8592-4

Printed from e-media with permission by:

Curran Associates, Inc.
57 Morehouse Lane
Red Hook, NY 12571

CURRAN ASSOCIATES INC. proceedings .com

Some format issues inherent in the e-media version may also appear in this print version.

Copyright© (2023) by the Association for Computational Linguistics
All rights reserved.

Printed with permission by Curran Associates, Inc. (2024)

For permission requests, please contact the Association for Computational Linguistics at the address below.

Association for Computational Linguistics
209 N. Eighth Street
Stroudsburg, Pennsylvania 18360

Phone: 1-570-476-8006
Fax: 1-570-476-0860

acl@aclweb.org

Additional copies of this publication are available from:

Curran Associates, Inc.
57 Morehouse Lane
Red Hook, NY 12571 USA
Phone: 845-758-0400
Fax: 845-758-2633
Email: curran@proceedings.com
Web: www.proceedings.com

EMNLP 2023

The 2023 Conference on Empirical Methods in Natural Language Processing

Tutorial Abstracts

December 6-10, 2023

©2023 Association for Computational Linguistics

Order copies of this and other ACL proceedings from:

Association for Computational Linguistics (ACL)
209 N. Eighth Street
Stroudsburg, PA 18360
USA
Tel: +1-570-476-8006
Fax: +1-570-476-0860
acl@aclweb.org

Introduction

Welcome to the Tutorials Session of EMNLP 2023.

The EMNLP tutorials session is organized to give conference attendees a comprehensive introduction by expert researchers to a variety of topics of importance drawn from our rapidly growing and changing research field.

This year, as has been the tradition over the past few years, the call, submission, reviewing and selection of tutorials were coordinated jointly for multiple conferences: EACL, ACL, and EMNLP. The committee followed a reviewing process that ensured that each of the 42 tutorial submissions received at least two reviews. The selection criteria included clarity, preparedness, novelty, timeliness, instructors' experience, likely audience, open access to the teaching materials, diversity (multilingualism, gender, age and geolocation) and the compatibility of preferred venues. A total of six tutorials were selected for EMNLP. We would like to thank the tutorial authors for their contributions and flexibility while organising the conference in a hybrid format. Finally, we would like to thank the conference organizers for effective collaboration, and in particular to the general chair Yuji Matsumoto.

We hope you enjoy the tutorials.

EMNLP 2023 Tutorial Co-chairs
Hassan Sajjad
Qi Zhang

Organizing Committee

General Chair

Yuji Matsumoto, RIKEN Center for Advanced Intelligence Project

Program Chairs

Houda Bouamor, Carnegie Mellon University in Qatar
Juan Pino, Meta
Kalika Bali, Microsoft Research Labs India

Tutorial Chairs

Qi Zhang, Fudan University
Hassan Sajjad, Dalhousie University

Table of Contents

Program

Wednesday, December 6, 2023

09:00 - 12:30 *Morning Session*

NLP+Vis: NLP Meets Visualization
Shafiq Joty, Enamul Hoque and Jesse Vig

Security Challenges in Natural Language Processing Models
Qiongkai Xu and Xuanli He

Designing, Evaluating, and Learning from Humans Interacting with NLP Models
Tongshuang Wu, Diyi Yang and Sebastin Santy

14:00 - 17:30 *Afternoon Session*

LLM-driven Instruction Following: Progresses and Concerns
Wenpeng Yin, Qinyuan Ye, Pengfei Liu, Xiang Ren and Hinrich Schütze

Mitigating Societal Harms in Large Language Models
Sachin Kumar, Vidhisha Balachandran, Lucille Njoo, Antonios Anastasopoulos and Yulia Tsvetkov

Creative Natural Language Generation
Tuhin Chakrabarty, Vishakh Padmakumar, He He and Nanyun Peng

NLP+Vis: NLP Meets Visualization

Shafiq Joty[♦♠], **Enamul Hoque**[♣], **Jesse Vig**[♦]
[♦]Salesforce Research, [♠]Nanyang Technological University, Singapore
[♣]York University, Canada
[♣]{enamulh}@yorku.ca
[♦]{sjoty, jvig}salesforce.com

Abstract

Natural language and visualization (Vis) are two powerful modalities of human communication. The goal of this tutorial is to push forward the agenda of tightly integrating these two modalities. To this end, the tutorial will introduce NLP+Vis with a focus on two main threads of work: (*i*) *NLP for Vis:* How to develop and adapt state-of-the-art NLP models for solving various visualization tasks? and (*ii*) *Vis for NLP*: How to leverage visualization techniques to interpret and explain complex NLP models effectively? The tutorial will first motivate why NLP+Vis is an important area of research and provide an overview of research topics on combining NLP and Vis techniques. Then an overview of state-of-the-art deep learning models for NLP will be covered. Next, we will provide an overview of applying visualization techniques to help make NLP models more interpretable and explainable. In the final part, we will focus on various application tasks at the intersection of NLP and Vis. We will conclude with an interactive discussion of future challenges for NLP+Vis applications. The audience will include researchers interested in applying NLP for visualizations as well as others who focus more generally at the intersection of machine learning and visualization.

1 Tutorial Overview

Natural language and visualization are two powerful modalities of human communication. Visualizations (Vis) are pervasive as they frequently appear in research papers, textbooks, reports, news articles, and webpages in various forms such as charts, diagrams, and infographics. While visualizations can be very effective in finding patterns, trends, and outliers in data, natural language can help explain the key points in visualizations (Obeid and Hoque, 2020) and enable users to express their complex information needs about data naturally (Setlur et al., 2016). For example, recent work on Chart Question Answering (QA) has demonstrated how NLP techniques can reduce perceptual and cognitive efforts by automatically answering complex reasoning questions about charts (Kantharaj et al., 2022; Masry et al., 2022; Lee et al., 2022) or by generating natural language summaries from charts (Shankar et al., 2022; Obeid and Hoque, 2020). We also refer the interested readers to Prof. Marti Hearst's keynote (link) at IEEE Vis'22 on how NLP can help Visualization.

Likewise, visualizations also have critical applications in the NLP domain. For example, visualization techniques can be leveraged to interpret neural NLP models and to visually explain how a model makes a prediction (Chatzimparmpas et al., 2020; Belinkov and Glass, 2019; Li et al., 2016; Tenney et al., 2020; Strobelt et al., 2018; Vig, 2019), and more recently to design *prompts* (i.e., natural language instructions accompanied with zero or few demonstrations) to effectively use large language models for zero-shot and few-shot task generalization (Strobelt et al., 2022).

The proposed tutorial will be aimed at those who would like to push forward the agenda of tightly integrating state-of-the-art NLP methods with visualizations. To this end, the tutorial aims to cover two primary topics of interest: (*i*) *NLP for Vis:* How to develop and adapt state-of-the-art NLP models for solving various visualization-related downstream tasks? (*ii*) *Vis for NLP*: How to leverage visualization techniques to interpret, explain and adapt complex NLP models effectively?

An overview of the tutorial is provided below:

- In the tutorial, we will first introduce the domain of NLP+Vis and provide an overview of various downstream tasks in this domain such as question answering with charts (e.g., Lee et al. (2022); Kantharaj et al. (2022); Masry et al. (2022)), science diagrams (Kembhavi et al., 2016), and infographics (Mathew et al., 2022), as well as natural language generation for visualizations (e.g., Shankar

Proceedings of the 2023 Conference on Empirical Methods in Natural Language Processing: Tutorial Abstracts, pages 1–6
December 6-10, 2023 ©2023 Association for Computational Linguistics

et al. (2022)) and text-to-chart (e.g., Wang et al. (2022)).

• Next, we will introduce the state-of-the-art deep learning methods from NLP which can be leveraged for solving various computational tasks for visualization research. In this part, we will cover topics such as Seq2Seq models, attentions and Transformers, pretraining and fine-tuning of large language models (e.g., GPT, BERT, BART, T5). We will also briefly cover emerging research in multimodal NLP (e.g., vision-language, data2NLP).

• Then, we will provide an overview of applying visualization techniques for making NLP models interpretable and explainable. In particular, we will cover how interactive visualization techniques can be leveraged to understand how the NLP model internally works and to explain how a specific prediction is made (Tenney et al., 2020; Wallace et al., 2019; Li et al., 2016; Spinner et al., 2019; Strobelt et al., 2018; Vig, 2019). We will also discuss the limitations and common pitfalls of applying visualization to model interpretability. Furthermore, we will cover how visualization techniques can be incorporated within interactive machine learning (Jiang et al., 2019) as well as prompt design (Strobelt et al., 2022) for zero-shot and few-shot generalization of large language models like GPT-3.

• In the final part, we will demonstrate applications of deep learning to NLP in the areas of visualizations including visual text analytics (Liu et al., 2018), chart question answering (e.g., Kantharaj et al. (2022); Masry et al. (2022)), conversational interfaces for visualizations (e.g., Hoque et al. (2017); Setlur et al. (2020)) and automatic data-driven story generation (e.g., Shi et al. (2020)). We will also cover NLP models for enhancing chart accessiblity and visualization literacy.

• The tutorial will conclude with an overview of future challenges in the domain of NLP+Vis.

The tutorial will facilitate interactive conversations with those who participate in person as well as those who will participate virtually. A website will host the details of the tutorial including slides and other resources such as suggested readings as well as web links to related datasets and code repositories.

1.1 Relevance to ACL Community

There are rapidly increasing research papers that are being published at the intersection of Vis and NLP, but to our knowledge, there has not been any tutorial at any ACL venues. We gave a related tutorial at the IEEE Vis 2022 conference. However, considering the target audience (visualization community), we restricted the content of that tutorial to *introductory* and the *NLP for Vis* topic only. In that sense, the scope of the proposed tutorial is much broader and covers mostly cutting-edge research. Given the growing interest in combining NLP and visualization and the recent advances in state-of-the-art deep learning techniques for NLP, we believe it is a very good time to arrange a tutorial on NLP+Vis.

1.2 Type of the Tutorial

Cutting-edge

1.3 Target Audience and Prerequisites

The tutorial will provide a gentle introduction to advanced deep learning models for NLP for solving various visualization-related tasks. Familiarity with Python (using numpy and PyTorch), Calculus, Linear Algebra, Basic Probability and Statistics and Machine Learning basics are expected.

While the primary target audience includes those interested in applying NLP techniques for visualization, the tutorial may be of interest to those who are more generally interested to work at the intersection of machine learning and visualization.

2 Outline: Tutorial Structure

2.1 Introduction [20 mins]

- What is NLP?
- What is Vis?
- Why NLP+Vis?
- An overview of research topics on combining NLP and Vis techniques
- An overview of the tutorial

2.2 NLP for Vis [70 mins]

- Encoder-decoder model
- Attention mechanism
- Transformer architecture

- Self-supervised learning (e.g., BERT, GPT, BART, T5)
- Applications (QA, Summarization, Dialog)
- Multi-modal deep learning
- Huggingface library

2.3 Coffee Break

2.4 Vis for NLP [25 mins]

- Intro to Vis for Interpretability
- Vis Tools and Use Cases
- Challenges and Limitations

2.5 NLP + Vis Applications [50 mins]

- Visual text analytics
- Natural language interfaces for visualizations
- ChartNLP (e.g., Chart question answering, Text2Chart)
- Natural language generation for visualization
- Automated data-driven storytelling
- NLP for chart accessibility
- NLP+Vis for inclusions (e.g., promote visualization Literacy)

2.6 Future Challenges [15 mins]

- Building benchmarks for training and evaluation
- Data annotation challenges
- Emerging applications

3 Breadth

30 - 40% of the tutorial materials will come from the work by the tutorial presenters, and the remaining 60 - 70% will come from other researchers' work.

4 Promoting Diversity and Inclusions

The tutorial integrates diversity and inclusion-related topics into the agenda. It is well-known that the lack of understanding of the important data aggravates inequalities in access to information among different user populations ranging from vulnerable and marginalized communities (e.g., refugees and indigenous communities) to people who face various physical and cognitive challenges (e.g., blindness, dementia, autism). For example, natural language can be helpful in improving chart accessibility (Sharif et al., 2022) and supporting novice users in exploring visualizations (Setlur et al., 2016). The tutorial will highlight possible application areas of NLP+Vis for promoting inclusions and diversity.

5 Instructors

Shafiq Joty[1] is a research director at Salesforce Research, and is also an Associate Professor (on leave) at NTU, Singapore. His work has primarily focused on developing language analysis tools and NLP applications. A significant part of his current research focuses on multilingual (machine translation, cross-lingual transfer), multimodal (visual-language learning, NLP+Vis, Code+NLP) NLP, interpretability and robustness of NLP models. His research contributed to 17 patents and more than 110 papers in top-tier NLP and ML conferences and journals including ACL, EMNLP, NAACL, NeurIPS, ICML, ICLR, CVPR, ECCV, ICCV, CL and JAIR. Shafiq served (or will serve) as a PC chair of SIGDIAL'23, an S/AC for ICLR-23, ACL'22, EMNLP'21, ACL'19-21, EMNLP'19, NAACL'21 and EACL'21 and an AE for ACL-RR. He gave tutorials at IEEE Vis'22, ACL'19, ICDM'18 and COLING'18, and taught deep learning for NLP,[2] a graduate-level NLP course, and an undergraduate NLP course at NTU.

Enamul Hoque[3] is an Associate Professor at York University where he directs the Intelligent Visualization Lab. Previously, he was a postdoctoral fellow in Computer Science at Stanford University. He received the Ph.D. degree in Computer Science from the University of British Columbia. His research focuses on combining information visualization and human-computer interaction with natural language processing to address the challenges of the information overload problem. Recently, he has worked on developing natural language interfaces for visualizations (e.g., (Hoque et al., 2017; Setlur et al., 2020)), automatic chart question answering (Kim et al., 2020; Kantharaj et al., 2022; Masry et al., 2022), chart retrieval (Hoque and Agrawala, 2019) and chart summarization (Shankar

[1] https://raihanjoty.github.io/

[2] https://ntunlpsg.github.io/ce7455_deep-nlp-20/

[3] https://www.yorku.ca/enamulh/

et al., 2022; Obeid and Hoque, 2020). He has also worked on developing visual text analytics to support the user's task of exploring and analyzing conversations (e.g., Hoque and Carenini (2014, 2015, 2016); Jasim et al. (2021)). Since his research is uniquely positioned at the intersection of information visualization, NLP, and HCI, he publishes at the major venues in each of these areas such as IEEE Vis, ACL, EMNLP, CHI, and UIST. He serves as an Area Chair for the ACL Rolling Review (2021-) and as a program committee member (2018-) for the IEEE Vis. He has also been teaching the graduate-level Information Visualization course at York University for the past 3 years.

Jesse Vig[4] is a lead research scientist at Salesforce Research working on NLP, explainable AI, and HCI. Much of his research has explored novel interpretability methods, ranging from causal analysis of language models (Vig et al., 2020) to attention interpretation in protein sequence models (Vig et al., 2021b). He developed the BertViz[5] (Vig, 2019) library for visualizing attention in Transformer models, as well as the SummVis (Vig et al., 2021a) and ProVis (Vig et al., 2021b) visualization tools. His work has appeared in NeurIPS, ICLR, IUI, UIST, ACL, NAACL, FAccT, and WWW, as well as the VISxAI and BlackBoxNLP workshops. Vig's research has been recognized with a Best Paper award at the Intelligent User Interfaces conference.

6 Audience Size

We expect 75 - 100 attendees. We gave a similar tutorial at the 2022 IEEE International Conference on Visualizations (Vis 2022), a top conference in data visualization. To the best of our knowledge, there were 600 - 800 attendees at that conference. The tutorials were run before the main conference. Despite this, our tutorial attracted a good number of attendees (~ 40).

7 Preferable Venues

Our preferable venues are in the following order: (*i*) ACL, (*ii*) EMNLP, and (*iii*) EACL

8 Technical Equipment

Projector and Internet access.

[4]

[5] https://github.com/jessevig/bertviz

9 Ethical Considerations

We have considered several ethical issues related to the topics of the tutorial. To respect the intellectual property of different dataset sources, we will only use publicly available charts that comply with their terms and conditions. To promote reproducibility, we will share the relevant code repositories and datasets. Finally, we will explain any possible misuse of techniques presented in the tutorial. In particular, we foresee one possible misuse of different models presented in the tutorial which is to spread misinformation. Currently, NLP model outputs tend to contain factual errors. Hence, if such model outputs are published without being corrected, they may mislead and misinform the general public.

References

Yonatan Belinkov and James Glass. 2019. Analysis Methods in Neural Language Processing: A Survey. *Transactions of the Association for Computational Linguistics*, 7:49–72.

Angelos Chatzimparmpas, Rafael M Martins, Ilir Jusufi, and Andreas Kerren. 2020. A survey of surveys on the use of visualization for interpreting machine learning models. *Information Visualization*, 19(3):207–233.

E Hoque and G Carenini. 2014. Convis: a visual text analytic system for exploring blog conversations. In *Proc. EuroVis*, pages 221–230.

Enamul Hoque and Maneesh Agrawala. 2019. Searching the visual style and structure of d3 visualizations. *IEEE transactions on visualization and computer graphics*, 26(1):1236–1245.

Enamul Hoque and Giuseppe Carenini. 2015. ConVisIT: Interactive topic modeling for exploring asynchronous online conversations. In *Proceedings of the 20th International Conference on Intelligent User Interfaces*, IUI '15, page 169–180, New York, NY, USA. Association for Computing Machinery.

Enamul Hoque and Giuseppe Carenini. 2016. MultiConvis: A visual text analytics system for exploring a collection of online conversations. In *Proc. IUI*, pages 96–107.

Enamul Hoque, Vidya Setlur, Melanie Tory, and Isaac Dykeman. 2017. Applying pragmatics principles for interaction with visual analytics. *IEEE Transactions on Visualization and Computer Graphics*, 24(1):309–318.

Mahmood Jasim, Enamul Hoque, Ali Sarvghad, and Narges Mahyar. 2021. Communitypulse: Facilitating community input analysis by surfacing hidden insights, reflections, and priorities. In *Designing Interactive Systems Conference 2021*, pages 846–863.

Liu Jiang, Shixia Liu, and Changjian Chen. 2019. Recent research advances on interactive machine learning. *Journal of Visualization*, 22(2):401–417.

Shankar Kantharaj, Xuan Long Do, Rixie Tiffany Ko Leong, Jia Qing Tan, Enamul Hoque, and Shafiq Joty. 2022. Opencqa: Open-ended question answering with charts. In *Proceedings of EMNLP (to appear)*.

Aniruddha Kembhavi, Mike Salvato, Eric Kolve, Minjoon Seo, Hannaneh Hajishirzi, and Ali Farhadi. 2016. A diagram is worth a dozen images. In *European conference on computer vision*, pages 235–251. Springer.

Dae Hyun Kim, Enamul Hoque, and Maneesh Agrawala. 2020. Answering questions about charts and generating visual explanations. In *Proceedings of the 2020 CHI Conference on Human Factors in Computing Systems*, pages 1–13.

Kenton Lee, Mandar Joshi, Iulia Turc, Hexiang Hu, Fangyu Liu, Julian Eisenschlos, Urvashi Khandelwal, Peter Shaw, Ming-Wei Chang, and Kristina Toutanova. 2022. Pix2struct: Screenshot parsing as pretraining for visual language understanding. *arXiv preprint arXiv:2210.03347*.

Jiwei Li, Xinlei Chen, Eduard Hovy, and Dan Jurafsky. 2016. Visualizing and understanding neural models in nlp. In *Proceedings of the 2016 Conference of the North American Chapter of the Association for Computational Linguistics: Human Language Technologies*, pages 681–691.

Shixia Liu, Xiting Wang, Christopher Collins, Wenwen Dou, Fangxin Ouyang, Mennatallah El-Assady, Liu Jiang, and Daniel A Keim. 2018. Bridging text visualization and mining: A task-driven survey. *IEEE transactions on visualization and computer graphics*, 25(7):2482–2504.

Ahmed Masry, Do Long, Jia Qing Tan, Shafiq Joty, and Enamul Hoque. 2022. ChartQA: A benchmark for question answering about charts with visual and logical reasoning. In *Findings of the Association for Computational Linguistics: ACL 2022*, pages 2263–2279.

Minesh Mathew, Viraj Bagal, Rubèn Tito, Dimosthenis Karatzas, Ernest Valveny, and CV Jawahar. 2022. Infographicvqa. In *Proceedings of the IEEE/CVF Winter Conference on Applications of Computer Vision*, pages 1697–1706.

Jason Obeid and Enamul Hoque. 2020. Chart-to-text: Generating natural language descriptions for charts by adapting the transformer model. In *Proceedings of the 13th International Conference on Natural Language Generation*, pages 138–147. Association for Computational Linguistics.

Vidya Setlur, Sarah E. Battersby, Melanie Tory, Rich Gossweiler, and Angel X. Chang. 2016. Eviza: A natural language interface for visual analysis. In *Proceedings of the 29th Annual Symposium on User Interface Software and Technology*, UIST 2016, pages 365–377, New York, NY, USA. ACM.

Vidya Setlur, Enamul Hoque, Dae Hyun Kim, and Angel X. Chang. 2020. Sneak pique: Exploring autocompletion as a data discovery scaffold for supporting visual analysis. In *Proceedings of the 33rd Annual ACM Symposium on User Interface Software and Technology*, UIST '20, page 966–978, New York, NY, USA. Association for Computing Machinery.

Kantharaj Shankar, Leong Rixie Tiffany Ko, Lin Xiang, Masry Ahmed, Thakkar Megh, Hoque Enamul, and Joty Shafiq. 2022. Chart-to-text: A large-scale benchmark for chart summarization. In *In Proceedings of the Annual Meeting of the Association for Computational Linguistics (ACL), 2022*.

Ather Sharif, Olivia H Wang, Alida T Muongchan, Katharina Reinecke, and Jacob O Wobbrock. 2022. Voxlens: Making online data visualizations accessible with an interactive javascript plug-in. In *CHI Conference on Human Factors in Computing Systems*, pages 1–19.

Danqing Shi, Xinyue Xu, Fuling Sun, Yang Shi, and Nan Cao. 2020. Calliope: Automatic visual data story generation from a spreadsheet. *IEEE Transactions on Visualization and Computer Graphics*, 27(2):453–463.

Thilo Spinner, Udo Schlegel, Hanna Schäfer, and Mennatallah El-Assady. 2019. explainer: A visual analytics framework for interactive and explainable machine learning. *IEEE transactions on visualization and computer graphics*, 26(1):1064–1074.

Hendrik Strobelt, Sebastian Gehrmann, Hanspeter Pfister, and Alexander M. Rush. 2018. Lstmvis: A tool for visual analysis of hidden state dynamics in recurrent neural networks. *IEEE Transactions on Visualization and Computer Graphics*, 24(1):667–676.

Hendrik Strobelt, Albert Webson, Victor Sanh, Benjamin Hoover, Johanna Beyer, Hanspeter Pfister, and Alexander M Rush. 2022. Interactive and visual prompt engineering for ad-hoc task adaptation with large language models. *IEEE transactions on visualization and computer graphics*.

Ian Tenney, James Wexler, Jasmijn Bastings, Tolga Bolukbasi, Andy Coenen, Sebastian Gehrmann, Ellen Jiang, Mahima Pushkarna, Carey Radebaugh, Emily Reif, and Ann Yuan. 2020. The language interpretability tool: Extensible, interactive visualizations and analysis for NLP models.

Jesse Vig. 2019. A multiscale visualization of attention in the transformer model. In *Proceedings of the 57th Annual Meeting of the Association for Computational Linguistics: System Demonstrations*, pages 37–42,

Florence, Italy. Association for Computational Linguistics.

Jesse Vig, Sebastian Gehrmann, Yonatan Belinkov, Sharon Qian, Daniel Nevo, Yaron Singer, and Stuart Shieber. 2020. Investigating gender bias in language models using causal mediation analysis. In *Advances in Neural Information Processing Systems*, volume 33, pages 12388–12401. Curran Associates, Inc.

Jesse Vig, Wojciech Kryscinski, Karan Goel, and Nazneen Rajani. 2021a. SummVis: Interactive visual analysis of models, data, and evaluation for text summarization. In *Proceedings of the 59th Annual Meeting of the Association for Computational Linguistics and the 11th International Joint Conference on Natural Language Processing: System Demonstrations*, pages 150–158, Online. Association for Computational Linguistics.

Jesse Vig, Ali Madani, Lav R. Varshney, Caiming Xiong, richard socher, and Nazneen Rajani. 2021b. BERTology meets biology: Interpreting attention in protein language models. In *International Conference on Learning Representations*.

Eric Wallace, Jens Tuyls, Junlin Wang, Sanjay Subramanian, Matt Gardner, and Sameer Singh. 2019. Allennlp interpret: A framework for explaining predictions of nlp models. pages 7–12.

Yun Wang, Zhitao Hou, Leixian Shen, Tongshuang Wu, Jiaqi Wang, He Huang, Haidong Zhang, and Dongmei Zhang. 2022. Towards natural language-based visualization authoring. *IEEE Transactions on Visualization and Computer Graphics*.

Security Challenges in Natural Language Processing Models

Qiongkai Xu[1,3] and **Xuanli He**[2]
[1] School of Computing and Information System, the University of Melbourne, Australia
[2] Department of Computer Science, University College London, United Kingdom
[3] School of Computing, FSE, Macquarie University, Australia
qiongkai.xu@mq.edu.au, xuanli.he@ucl.ac.uk

Abstract

Large-scale natural language processing models have been developed and integrated into numerous applications, given the advantage of their remarkable performance. Nonetheless, the security concerns associated with these models prevent the widespread adoption of these black-box machine learning models. In this tutorial, we will dive into three emerging security issues in NLP research, i.e., backdoor attacks, private data leakage, and imitation attacks. These threats will be introduced in accordance with their threatening usage scenarios, attack methodologies, and defense technologies.

1 Tutorial Content

1.1 Introduction

Large-scale natural language processing models have recently garnered substantial attention due to their exceptional performance. This promotes a significant proliferation in the development and deployment of black-box NLP APIs across a wide range of applications. Simultaneously, an expanding body of research has revealed profound security vulnerabilities associated with these black-box APIs, encompassing issues such as dysfunctional failures (Gu et al., 2017; Dai et al., 2019; Huang et al., 2023), concerns related to privacy and data leakage (Coavoux et al., 2018; Carlini et al., 2021), and infringements on intellectual property (Wallace et al., 2020; Xu et al., 2022). Those security challenges can lead to issues like data misuse, financial loss, reputation damage, legal disputes, and more. It is worth noting that these security vulnerabilities are not mere theoretical assumptions. Previous research has demonstrated that both commercial APIs and publicly available models can be easily compromised (Wallace et al., 2020; Carlini et al., 2021; Xu et al., 2022). This tutorial aims to provide a comprehensive overview of the latest research concerning security challenges in NLP models.

1.2 Security Challenges in NLP

This section will delineate three prevalent security challenges encountered in NLP research and applications. These include (1) backdoor attacks, (2) privacy concerns and data leakage, and (3) imitation attacks. For each of these challenges, we will first commence by introducing their threat model in real-world applications. Subsequently, we will delve into the techniques used to execute these attacks, illustrating their impact on vulnerable applications. Finally, we will discuss the countermeasures and defense technologies available to mitigate these attacks.

Adversarial and Backdoor Attacks. Our discussion commences with adversarial attacks in the context of NLP tasks. These attacks involve the manipulation of inputs to compromise the performance of a target model (Alzantot et al., 2018; Ebrahimi et al., 2018; Li et al., 2018). More specifically, by altering specific characters or words, it becomes possible to deceive a text classifier into assigning an incorrect label. This research underscores the inherent vulnerability of trained NLP models. A notable subset of these attacks is the backdoor attack, where the victim model is induced to associate misbehavior with specific triggers (Dai et al., 2019). During the inference stage, poisoned models exhibit normal behavior on clean inputs, but their misbehavior is triggered when malicious patterns are presented. Those malevolent actions can range from deceiving text classifiers (Dai et al., 2019; Kurita et al., 2020) to mistranslating neutral phrases into controversial ones (Xu et al., 2021).

In the literature, there exist two primary strategies for embedding backdoor triggers: (1) data poisoning and (2) weight poisoning. Data poisoning seeks to infiltrate triggers into a victim model by poisoning a small fraction of the training data,

Proceedings of the 2023 Conference on Empirical Methods in Natural Language Processing: Tutorial Abstracts, pages 7–12
December 6-10, 2023 ©2023 Association for Computational Linguistics

as demonstrated in various studies (Dai et al., 2019; Chen et al., 2021; Qi et al., 2021b; Wang et al., 2021; Xu et al., 2021). Regarding weight poisoning, attackers surreptitiously integrate the triggers into the victim model's weights (Kurita et al., 2020; Li et al., 2021; Yang et al., 2021a) or their embedding dictionary (Huang et al., 2023). It is noteworthy that the majority of backdoor attacks have centered on supervised learning. However, with the growing prominence of instruction tuning (Ouyang et al., 2022; Wei et al., 2022), we will delve into the manipulation of large language models through instruction tuning poisoning in subsequent discussions (Wan et al., 2023; Xu et al., 2023; Shu et al., 2023).

In conjunction with the literature on backdoor attacks, we will cover multiple defensive approaches that aim at mitigating the vulnerabilities caused by these attacks. Depending on the level of access to the training data, these defensive measures can be categorized into two types: (1) *training-stage* defense and (2) *test-stage* defense. The former method aims at identifying poisoned data by analyzing the anomalous characteristics of the training data (Sun et al., 2021; He et al., 2023b). The latter approach leverages external tools (Qi et al., 2021a) or the victim language models themselves (Yang et al., 2021b; Chen et al., 2022; He et al., 2023a) to either remove the triggers or entirely discard the poisoned data samples during the inference.

Privacy and Data Leakage. Another challenge in NLP models is the potential risk of disclosing data, particularly sensitive content, to untrustworthy parties. A recent widely recognized example is the capability of pre-trained language models, e.g., GPT-2, to generate sentences containing sensitive information when provided with carefully designed prompts (Carlini et al., 2021). Another concern revolves around the possibility that certain information from the training data is inferred through the model's parameters or the gradient updates, such as membership inference and text data recovery (Melis et al., 2019; Gupta et al., 2022). These types of attacks pose significant challenges to collaborative learning of language models (Yang et al., 2019).

Privacy and data leakage present a contentious challenge in NLP models. In this discussion, we will introduce technologies aimed at addressing these concerns, including (1) unlearning specific private training data, known as machine unlearning (Bourtoule et al., 2021), (2) methods for identifying the generated outputs that may contain sensitive attributes (Xu et al., 2020) and (3) techniques that obscure the intermediate representation of NLP models, such as the application of differential privacy (Lyu et al., 2020; Shi et al., 2022).

Imitation Attack. The final security challenge within our scope will be the imitation attack on NLP models. With the advancement of NLP models, particularly large pre-trained language models, companies have encapsulated exceptional models into commercial APIs, serving millions of end-users. In order to foster a profitable market, service providers commonly implement pay-as-you-use policies for those APIs. To circumvent service charges, a seminal work (Tramèr et al., 2016) proposed the imitation of the functionality of commercial APIs by relying on predictions from those APIs. Subsequent research has revealed vulnerabilities associated with imitation attacks that extend beyond the violation of intellectual property, e.g., one can employ the imitation model to craft transferable adversarial examples capable of deceiving the victim model as well (Wallace et al., 2020; He et al., 2021). Moreover, the interaction between the victim model and the imitator can lead to significant privacy breaches (He et al., 2022a). Furthermore, Xu et al. (2022) demonstrate that imitation models can outperform the imitated victim models, particularly in the context of domain adaptation and model ensemble.

Several studies have devised a range of defensive strategies to mitigate those security threats. Given that imitation attacks depend on the predictions made by victim models, one straightforward solution involves manipulating these predictions such that the imitation models are trained with partial or potentially deceptive information. We will delve into the details of how this has been achieved in text classification and generation problems, including techniques such as customizing and perturbing predicted label distributions (Xu et al., 2022; He et al., 2022a). Additionally, we will explore recent advancements in watermarking technologies for intellectual property protection (Krishna et al., 2020; He et al., 2022b,c; Zhao et al., 2023)

2 Relevance and Importance to Computational Linguistic Community

Large-scale language models have achieved significant performance in many NLP tasks, with many applications now reliant on those advanced NLP models. However, any uncontrolled misconduct, the inadvertent disclosure of private training data, or potential leaks of model intellectual property could result in substantial financial and social consequences. The imperative to guide the future development of NLP models is shifting from mere task performance to a growing emphasis on the security and ethical concerns of these models. Machine learning models, especially large-scale deep learning models, remain somewhat inscrutable to human comprehension. This opacity raises the challenges in identifying and addressing potential risks associated with these models without comprehensive explanations and a deep understanding of their inner workings. In order to inspire broader discussion and foster research efforts in the domain of security in NLP, this tutorial is dedicated to presenting the principle security challenges in modern natural language processing models. This will include exploration of their threat models, attack methodologies, and defense technologies.

3 Tutorial Information

Tutorial Outline The tutorial is expected to be 3.5 hours, including a half-hour coffee break.

1. Introduction (15 mins)
2. Backdoor Attack (50 min, by Xuanli He)
   (a) Problem definition and motivation;
   (b) Adversarial and Backdoor Attacks on NLP models;
   (c) Defense techniques against backdoor attacks.
3. Privacy and Data Leakage (50 min, by Qiongkai Xu)
   (a) Problem definition and motivation;
   (b) Privacy Leakage in NLP models;
   (c) Data Leakage in NLP models;
   (d) Defense techniques against privacy and data Leakage.
4. Imitation Attack (50 min, by Qiongkai Xu and/or Xuanli He)
   (a) Problem motivation and definition;
   (b) Imitation attack and subsequent attacks;
   (c) Defense techniques against imitation attack.
5. Conclusion and Future Trends (15 mins)

Topic Breadth. Our expectation is that approximately 30% of the content will be drawn from the work of the instructors, while the remaining 70% will be sourced from contributions made by various other researchers. The materials we intend to cover include papers from both academia and industry.

Ethical Considerations. In this tutorial, we shed light on various vulnerabilities found in contemporary NLP models. Our intention in discussing these vulnerabilities is not to endorse any form of attack. Rather, our objective is to emphasize the importance of responsible AI practices in both academic and industrial contexts. Through this approach, we can harness the progress made in AI while concurrently upholding security, privacy, and ethical considerations.

Open Accessibility. We intend to ensure that all instructional materials are available online.[1] Moreover, we grant permission to include slides and video recordings in the ACL anthology.

4 Prerequisites for the Attendees

This tutorial is designed to cater to the needs of both NLP researchers and students in academia, as well as industrial practitioners with an interest in security & privacy in NLP, model explanation, and related areas. While a basic understanding of Machine Learning is beneficial, it is not an obligatory prerequisite.

5 Reading List

- Backdoor Attack (Gu et al., 2017; Dai et al., 2019; Kurita et al., 2020)
- Privacy and Data Leakage (Melis et al., 2019; Carlini et al., 2021; He et al., 2022a)
- Imitation Attack (Wallace et al., 2020; Xu et al., 2022)
- Defense using differential privacy (Lyu et al., 2020; Shi et al., 2022), machine unlearning (Bourtoule et al., 2021), and watermarking (He et al., 2022b)

6 Presenters

Dr. Qiongkai Xu, Research Fellow on Security in NLP, School of Computing and Infor-

[1] The resources pertaining to this tutorial are available at `https://emnlp2023-nlp-security.github.io/`.

mation System, the University of Melbourne, Australia.[2]
https://xuqiongkai.github.io
https://scholar.google.com/citations?user=wCer2WUAAAAJ

His recent research interest lies in auditing machine learning models, namely 1) privacy and security issues in ML/NLP models and 2) new evaluation paradigms for ML/NLP models. He has published more than 30 papers, with more than 10 of them on the topic of privacy and security in NLP.

Dr. Xuanli He, Research Fellow, Department of Computer Science, University College London, UK.
https://xlhex.github.io/
https://scholar.google.com/citations?user=TU8t0iAAAAAJ&hl

His recent research lies in an intersection between deep learning and natural language processing, with an emphasis on robustness and security in NLP models. He has published more than 10 top-tier conference papers about security in NLP models.

Acknowledgments

We thank Trevor Cohn, Benjamin I. P. Rubinstein, Lingjuan Lyu, and anonymous reviewers for their insightful suggestions, discussion, and comments on this tutorial and involved related work.

References

Moustafa Alzantot, Yash Sharma, Ahmed Elgohary, Bo-Jhang Ho, Mani Srivastava, and Kai-Wei Chang. 2018. Generating natural language adversarial examples. In *Proceedings of the 2018 Conference on Empirical Methods in Natural Language Processing*, pages 2890–2896, Brussels, Belgium. Association for Computational Linguistics.

Lucas Bourtoule, Varun Chandrasekaran, Christopher A Choquette-Choo, Hengrui Jia, Adelin Travers, Baiwu Zhang, David Lie, and Nicolas Papernot. 2021. Machine unlearning. In *2021 IEEE Symposium on Security and Privacy (SP)*, pages 141–159. IEEE.

Nicholas Carlini, Florian Tramer, Eric Wallace, Matthew Jagielski, Ariel Herbert-Voss, Katherine Lee, Adam Roberts, Tom Brown, Dawn Song, Ulfar Erlingsson, et al. 2021. Extracting training data from large language models. In *30th USENIX Security Symposium (USENIX Security 21)*, pages 2633–2650.

Sishuo Chen, Wenkai Yang, Zhiyuan Zhang, Xiaohan Bi, and Xu Sun. 2022. Expose backdoors on the way: A feature-based efficient defense against textual backdoor attacks.

Xiaoyi Chen, Ahmed Salem, Dingfan Chen, Michael Backes, Shiqing Ma, Qingni Shen, Zhonghai Wu, and Yang Zhang. 2021. Badnl: Backdoor attacks against nlp models with semantic-preserving improvements. In *Annual Computer Security Applications Conference*, pages 554–569.

Maximin Coavoux, Shashi Narayan, and Shay B Cohen. 2018. Privacy-preserving neural representations of text. In *Proceedings of the 2018 Conference on Empirical Methods in Natural Language Processing*, pages 1–10.

Jiazhu Dai, Chuanshuai Chen, and Yufeng Li. 2019. A backdoor attack against lstm-based text classification systems. *IEEE Access*, 7:138872–138878.

Javid Ebrahimi, Anyi Rao, Daniel Lowd, and Dejing Dou. 2018. HotFlip: White-box adversarial examples for text classification. In *Proceedings of the 56th Annual Meeting of the Association for Computational Linguistics (Volume 2: Short Papers)*, pages 31–36, Melbourne, Australia. Association for Computational Linguistics.

Tianyu Gu, Brendan Dolan-Gavitt, and Siddharth Garg. 2017. Badnets: Identifying vulnerabilities in the machine learning model supply chain. *arXiv preprint arXiv:1708.06733*.

Samyak Gupta, Yangsibo Huang, Zexuan Zhong, Tianyu Gao, Kai Li, and Danqi Chen. 2022. Recovering private text in federated learning of language models. In *Advances in Neural Information Processing Systems (NeurIPS)*.

Xuanli He, Chen Chen, Lingjuan Lyu, and Qiongkai Xu. 2022a. Extracted bert model leaks more information than you think! In *Proceedings of the 2022 Conference on Empirical Methods in Natural Language Processing*.

Xuanli He, Lingjuan Lyu, Lichao Sun, and Qiongkai Xu. 2021. Model extraction and adversarial transferability, your BERT is vulnerable! In *Proceedings of the 2021 Conference of the North American Chapter of the Association for Computational Linguistics: Human Language Technologies*, pages 2006–2012, Online. Association for Computational Linguistics.

Xuanli He, Jun Wang, Benjamin Rubinstein, and Trevor Cohn. 2023a. IMBERT: Making BERT immune to insertion-based backdoor attacks. In *Proceedings of the 3rd Workshop on Trustworthy Natural Language Processing (TrustNLP 2023)*, pages 287–301, Toronto, Canada. Association for Computational Linguistics.

Xuanli He, Qiongkai Xu, Lingjuan Lyu, Fangzhao Wu, and Chenguang Wang. 2022b. Protecting intellectual property of language generation apis with lexical watermark. *Proceedings of the AAAI Conference on Artificial Intelligence*, pages 10758–10766.

[2]He is now at Macquarie University as a lecturer.

Xuanli He, Qiongkai Xu, Jun Wang, Benjamin Rubinstein, and Trevor Cohn. 2023b. Mitigating backdoor poisoning attacks through the lens of spurious correlation. *arXiv preprint arXiv:2305.11596*.

Xuanli He, Qiongkai Xu, Yi Zeng, Lingjuan Lyu, Fangzhao Wu, Jiwei Li, and Ruoxi Jia. 2022c. CATER: Intellectual property protection on text generation APIs via conditional watermarks. In *Advances in Neural Information Processing Systems*.

Yujin Huang, Terry Yue Zhuo, Qiongkai Xu, Han Hu, Xingliang Yuan, and Chunyang Chen. 2023. Training-free lexical backdoor attacks on language models. In *Proceedings of the ACM Web Conference 2023*, pages 2198–2208.

Kalpesh Krishna, Gaurav Singh Tomar, Ankur P. Parikh, Nicolas Papernot, and Mohit Iyyer. 2020. Thieves on sesame street! model extraction of bert-based apis. In *International Conference on Learning Representations*.

Keita Kurita, Paul Michel, and Graham Neubig. 2020. Weight poisoning attacks on pretrained models. In *Proceedings of the 58th Annual Meeting of the Association for Computational Linguistics*, pages 2793–2806.

Jinfeng Li, Shouling Ji, Tianyu Du, Bo Li, and Ting Wang. 2018. Textbugger: Generating adversarial text against real-world applications. *arXiv preprint arXiv:1812.05271*.

Linyang Li, Demin Song, Xiaonan Li, Jiehang Zeng, Ruotian Ma, and Xipeng Qiu. 2021. Backdoor attacks on pre-trained models by layerwise weight poisoning. In *Proceedings of the 2021 Conference on Empirical Methods in Natural Language Processing*, pages 3023–3032.

Lingjuan Lyu, Xuanli He, and Yitong Li. 2020. Differentially private representation for nlp: Formal guarantee and an empirical study on privacy and fairness. In *Findings of the Association for Computational Linguistics: EMNLP 2020*, pages 2355–2365.

Luca Melis, Congzheng Song, Emiliano De Cristofaro, and Vitaly Shmatikov. 2019. Exploiting unintended feature leakage in collaborative learning. In *2019 IEEE symposium on security and privacy (SP)*, pages 691–706. IEEE.

Long Ouyang, Jeffrey Wu, Xu Jiang, Diogo Almeida, Carroll Wainwright, Pamela Mishkin, Chong Zhang, Sandhini Agarwal, Katarina Slama, Alex Ray, et al. 2022. Training language models to follow instructions with human feedback. *Advances in Neural Information Processing Systems*, 35:27730–27744.

Fanchao Qi, Yangyi Chen, Mukai Li, Yuan Yao, Zhiyuan Liu, and Maosong Sun. 2021a. Onion: A simple and effective defense against textual backdoor attacks. In *Proceedings of the 2021 Conference on Empirical Methods in Natural Language Processing*, pages 9558–9566.

Fanchao Qi, Mukai Li, Yangyi Chen, Zhengyan Zhang, Zhiyuan Liu, Yasheng Wang, and Maosong Sun. 2021b. Hidden killer: Invisible textual backdoor attacks with syntactic trigger. In *Proceedings of the 59th Annual Meeting of the Association for Computational Linguistics and the 11th International Joint Conference on Natural Language Processing (Volume 1: Long Papers)*, pages 443–453.

Weiyan Shi, Aiqi Cui, Evan Li, Ruoxi Jia, and Zhou Yu. 2022. Selective differential privacy for language modeling. In *Proceedings of the 2022 Conference of the North American Chapter of the Association for Computational Linguistics: Human Language Technologies*, pages 2848–2859, Seattle, United States. Association for Computational Linguistics.

Manli Shu, Jiongxiao Wang, Chen Zhu, Jonas Geiping, Chaowei Xiao, and Tom Goldstein. 2023. On the exploitability of instruction tuning. *arXiv preprint arXiv:2306.17194*.

Xiaofei Sun, Jiwei Li, Xiaoya Li, Ziyao Wang, Tianwei Zhang, Han Qiu, Fei Wu, and Chun Fan. 2021. A general framework for defending against backdoor attacks via influence graph. *arXiv preprint arXiv:2111.14309*.

Florian Tramèr, Fan Zhang, Ari Juels, Michael K Reiter, and Thomas Ristenpart. 2016. Stealing machine learning models via prediction {APIs}. In *25th USENIX security symposium (USENIX Security 16)*, pages 601–618.

Eric Wallace, Mitchell Stern, and Dawn Song. 2020. Imitation attacks and defenses for black-box machine translation systems. In *Proceedings of the 2020 Conference on Empirical Methods in Natural Language Processing (EMNLP)*, pages 5531–5546.

Alexander Wan, Eric Wallace, Sheng Shen, and Dan Klein. 2023. Poisoning language models during instruction tuning. In *International Conference on Machine Learning*.

Jun Wang, Chang Xu, Francisco Guzmán, Ahmed El-Kishky, Yuqing Tang, Benjamin Rubinstein, and Trevor Cohn. 2021. Putting words into the system's mouth: A targeted attack on neural machine translation using monolingual data poisoning. In *Findings of the Association for Computational Linguistics: ACL-IJCNLP 2021*, pages 1463–1473.

Jason Wei, Maarten Bosma, Vincent Zhao, Kelvin Guu, Adams Wei Yu, Brian Lester, Nan Du, Andrew M. Dai, and Quoc V Le. 2022. Finetuned language models are zero-shot learners. In *International Conference on Learning Representations*.

Chang Xu, Jun Wang, Yuqing Tang, Francisco Guzmán, Benjamin IP Rubinstein, and Trevor Cohn. 2021. A targeted attack on black-box neural machine translation with parallel data poisoning. In *Proceedings of the Web Conference 2021*, pages 3638–3650.

Jiashu Xu, Mingyu Derek Ma, Fei Wang, Chaowei Xiao, and Muhao Chen. 2023. Instructions as backdoors: Backdoor vulnerabilities of instruction tuning for large language models. *arXiv preprint arXiv:2305.14710*.

Qiongkai Xu, Xuanli He, Lingjuan Lyu, Lizhen Qu, and Gholamreza Haffari. 2022. Student surpasses teacher: Imitation attack for black-box NLP APIs. In *Proceedings of the 29th International Conference on Computational Linguistics*, pages 2849–2860, Gyeongju, Republic of Korea. International Committee on Computational Linguistics.

Qiongkai Xu, Lizhen Qu, Zeyu Gao, and Gholamreza Haffari. 2020. Personal information leakage detection in conversations. In *Proceedings of the 2020 Conference on Empirical Methods in Natural Language Processing (EMNLP)*, pages 6567–6580.

Qiang Yang, Yang Liu, Yong Cheng, Yan Kang, Tianjian Chen, and Han Yu. 2019. Federated learning. *Synthesis Lectures on Artificial Intelligence and Machine Learning*, 13(3):1–207.

Wenkai Yang, Lei Li, Zhiyuan Zhang, Xuancheng Ren, Xu Sun, and Bin He. 2021a. Be careful about poisoned word embeddings: Exploring the vulnerability of the embedding layers in NLP models. In *Proceedings of the 2021 Conference of the North American Chapter of the Association for Computational Linguistics: Human Language Technologies*, pages 2048–2058, Online. Association for Computational Linguistics.

Wenkai Yang, Yankai Lin, Peng Li, Jie Zhou, and Xu Sun. 2021b. Rap: Robustness-aware perturbations for defending against backdoor attacks on nlp models. In *Proceedings of the 2021 Conference on Empirical Methods in Natural Language Processing*, pages 8365–8381.

Xuandong Zhao, Yu-Xiang Wang, and Lei Li. 2023. Protecting language generation models via invisible watermarking. *arXiv preprint arXiv:2302.03162*.

Designing, Learning from, and Evaluating Human-AI Interactions

Tongshuang Wu[†] **Diyi Yang**[‡] **Sebastin Santy**[±]
[†] Carnegie Mellon University [‡] Stanford University [±] University of Washington

1 Introduction

With the rapid advancement of natural language processing (NLP) research, there are numerous applications across a wide range of domains that require models to interact with humans — for example, chatbots responding to human inquiries (Thoppilan et al., 2022), machine translation systems aiding human translators (Santy et al., 2021), designers prompting Large Language Models for co-creation (Gero et al., 2022) or prototyping AI-infused applications (Park et al., 2022). In each of these cases, (timely) human interaction has been the key to the success; and any potential misconceptions or differences introduced to this interaction process might lead to error cascades at later stages (Sambasivan et al., 2021). Such interaction involves a lot of design choices *around* models — the sensitivity of interfaces (Amershi et al., 2019) and modalities (Ravichander et al., 2021), the impact of questions during human evaluation (Clark et al., 2021), or incorporating steer-ability in models (Dathathri et al., 2019).

These choices are equally (if not more) important compared to the algorithms or datasets, but they are often undervalued and sometimes even considered a trivial part of the equation. In fact, while many of these topics have been extensively investigated in Human-Computer Interaction (HCI), they have only recently gained sufficient attention in NLP. NLP researchers entering the interaction world typically have to go through a steep learning curve before they can fully utilize the best practices from HCI, resulting in some unintentional decisions that have adversely affected the reproducibility of earlier work (Clark et al., 2021).

In this tutorial, we aim to provide a systematic and up-to-date overview of key considerations and effective approaches for studying human-NLP model interactions. Interactions can take various forms depending on the stage of model development and the human involved; For example, NLP researchers and developers may interactively debug models during development, crowdworkers may participate in data annotation, etc.Our tutorial will focus specifically on the scenario where *end users* — lay people and domain experts who try to use and benefit from NLP models — interact or collaborate with deployed models (Wu & Bansal et al., 2021).

Throughout the tutorial, we will use four case studies (on model-assisted decision making, machine-aided translation, dialog systems, and prompting) to cover three major themes: (1) how to conduct usability ***evaluations*** to ensure that models are capable of interacting with humans; (2) how to ***design*** user interfaces (UIs) and interaction mechanisms that allow end users to easily access NLP models; (3) how to ***learn from*** and improve NLP models through human interaction. We will ground our discussion in HCI best practices, highlighting current challenges and future directions.

2 Tutorial Outline

This will be a **three-hour tutorial** devoted to the **cutting-edge topic** of *Designing, Learning from, and Evaluating Human-AI Interaction.* Each theme will take 35 mins, followed by 10 mins for Q&A and 10 mins for a break. Each part includes an overview of the corresponding topics, widely used methods, and a deep dive into a set of representative NLP and HCI work. In the last 15 minutes, we will conclude our tutorial by highlighting challenges and research opportunities in the field.

2.1 Walkthrough Case Studies

For consistency, we will use four case studies throughout the tutorial. They demonstrate how humans and models would play different roles, sometimes working together, sometimes supporting one another. We use them to discuss interaction initiation, usability priorities, etc.

Proceedings of the 2023 Conference on Empirical Methods in Natural Language Processing: Tutorial Abstracts, pages 13–18
December 6-10, 2023 ©2023 Association for Computational Linguistics

Model-assisted decision making. NLP Models are quite often used when making decisions such in clinical settings. In this setup, humans and AI collaborate towards a common goal, with the hope that each makes a decisions that they are best suited to make. It is an example of how standard evaluation may not translate to model usability in an interaction setup, because accurate models may not be complementary to human strengths (Bansal et al., 2021). Meanwhile, numerous studies have explored how humans would interact with classifiers making recommendations given various visual representations of model outputs and various forms of model explanations (e.g., Wu & Bansal et al., 2021; Gonzalez et al., 2020). This more mature and well-researched scenario will be used to give an overarching introduction on evaluation (§2.2) and interaction design (§2.3).

Machine-aided Translation. This instead illustrates a situation where humans take the initiative while the model provides assistance. With humans making the final judge on model usefulness, various evaluation dimensions are affected. For example, humans would deem a model useful even if they are partially correct (Green et al., 2014b) and different user groups get different benefits (Santy et al., 2021). Meanwhile, users' needs and perceptions on the model also affect their use patterns, e.g., they may only use models for keyword translation if model outputs are not fluent (Green et al., 2013, 2014a), which in turn points to future model improvement. We will use this case study to review the importance of human understanding and tracking in evaluation and learning (§2.4).

Dialog systems. Chatbot/dialog system is another early adoption of NLP techniques that also fall under models supporting humans. It represents the use case where evaluation is dynamic (1) the model performance is easily swayed by human responses and can hardly be measured on benchmark datasets (Li et al., 2021), (2) the model has to balance multiple criteria like interestingness, informativeness, etc. which could be subjective for different user groups (Thoppilan et al., 2022), (3) it is essential to implement fallback options (e.g., responses like "sorry I didn't understand" that's built around the model at the UI level) when the model does not behave as expected or safety modules when there is potential for controversiality (Kim et al., 2022). These properties also make dialog systems an ideal testbed for discussing UI designs (§2.3) and personalization (§2.4).

Prompting Large Lanuge Models Recently, large Language Models has made NLP models more accessible to end users, and has led to the emergence of a brand new interaction mechanism — prompting. Prompting perhaps represents a rare case where humans are "supporting" the model, i.e., they try to search for optimal instructions that maximize model performances on certain tasks. We will review various recent papers on prompting strategies (e.g., chaining (Wu et al., 2022), defining shareable prompt templates (Dang et al., 2022), inducing personas from LLMs (Reynolds and McDonell, 2021)), with an emphasis on the trade-off of expressiveness and learning curve (Jiang et al., 2022), and the potential of learning from user feedback (e.g., InstructGPT (Ouyang et al., 2022)). We will also emphasize on the differences between LLMs (which can respond to arbitrary human input text) and other modeling structures (which make more assumptions on possible text inputs).

2.2 Theme 1: Evaluate Model Usability

The first part of our tutorial will focus on evaluating NLP model usability. As mentioned in §2.1, NLP models that interact with (make suggestions to, have conversations with) humans need to go beyond accuracy (Ribeiro et al., 2020; Bhatt et al., 2021). User interaction experiences are affected by human-centered metrics such as safety, latency, faithfulness, responsiveness, etc. We refer to these dimensions as *usability evaluation*. In most cases, these evaluations are conducted on human subjects. Users would interact with both a target (experiment) model and a baseline (control) model, and compare them on effectiveness, usefulness, etc. through self-rating. The usability evaluations determine whether a model is ready for actual use. Unfortunately, their results are often easily swayed by arbitrary design choices (e.g., the survey question, the task instruction) (Roopa and Rani, 2012), making them unreliable.

This tutorial will guide the participants to design rigorous usability evaluations. Following the evaluation categorization in HCI (Kuniavsky, 2003), we will cover (1) survey design, (2) think-aloud protocol, (3) cognitive walkthrough, and (4) Experimentation and A/B testing. We will also discuss useful qualitative (e.g., Likert Scale results) and quantitative metrics (e.g., retrieving interaction speed from user clickstream (Lee et al., 2022)), best use scenario and typical design pitfalls for each approach (e.g., leading questions in *survey design*).

Besides methodologies, this tutorial will also discuss the user group selection (Olsen Jr, 2007): (1) the potential impact of running studies on crowdsourcing platforms (where motivating participants is challenging and denoising is essential), in the lab (where graduate students are frequently used but can only represent a biased distribution), and in the actual deployment environment (which is costly); (2) the importance of identifying the targeted user group and achieving good coverage.

2.3 Theme 2: Interaction Design

Usability evaluation can help judge whether a model is usable, but user interfaces are still needed to make it user friendly. This part concerns the interface and interaction design, with two focuses:

(1) *Communication*, i.e., what inputs the model should take from humans and how to present the results. We will present different modes of human input (e.g., Natural Language input vs. traditional WIMP interfaces) and discuss their trade-offs (Wang et al., 2022). Additionally, we will discuss the desiderata for visualizing NLP model training information, their predictions, uncertainties, and (where applicable) explanations, as well as the impact of design choice (Khadpe et al., 2020). In addition, we will discuss how NLP models can have a design bias that make them difficult for people from different demographics (culture, language, age, gender), and how interactions may rectify the issues to some extent.

(2) *Initiation*, i.e., how the NLP model and the human can take the leading roles interchangeably. We will ground our discussion on the mixed-initiative interaction mechanism (Avula et al., 2022) — a flexible interaction strategy in which each agent contributes what it is best suited at the most appropriate time — and discuss how model initiations impact the perceived model usefulness (Avula et al., 2022; Santy et al., 2019), and how human initiations may be used as not only a driving force on achieving human goals (Oh et al., 2018), but also a fallback option when the model does not behave as expected (Lee et al., 2022).

2.4 Theme 3: Learn from Interactions

As users interact with NLP models, they generate rich signals that reveal model incorrectness and point to future model improvements (Krishna et al., 2022). For example, users may submit explicit feedback (e.g., users flagging a translation as incorrect) (Cabrera et al., 2021; Stiennon et al., 2020), or their clickstream may implicitly reflect their expectations on a model (e.g., when they revise a model-generated text after accepting the suggestion (Lee et al., 2022)).

Here, we review different types of human feedback that can be naturally retrieved from human interactions, as well as different modeling approaches to incorporate human feedback. Building on the survey from our presenter team (Wang et al., 2021), we will review recent studies that incorporate human feedback with respect to their goals, human interactions, and feedback learning methods, with a focus on example-based feedback (Wallace et al., 2019, e.g.,) and reinforce learning (Ouyang et al., 2022; Stiennon et al., 2020). In particular, we will also re-emphasize how the feedback can be retrieved through the methods introduced in §2.3. Additionally, to help researchers make practical use of these methods, we will discuss the potential trade-offs between intuitiveness vs. expressiveness (e.g., labeling functions in weak supervision (Ratner et al., 2016) might be more scalable but more difficult than labeling a single counterexample (Wallace et al., 2019)).

2.5 Breadth

While we will give pointers to dozens of relevant papers, we plan to cover around 7-8 research papers in close detail. Only 1-2 of the "deep dive" papers will come from the presenter team.

2.6 A Comparison with Relevant Tutorials

Given the rising awareness of human-centered NLP (a special theme at NAACL 2022), it is not surprising that some tutorials have already touched on some relevant topics. To the best of our knowledge, two tutorials that are closest to ours are: (1) *Case Studies in Benchmark Data Collection* at EMNLP 2021[1]) which uses six case studies to present a wide variety of data collection crowdsourcing methods and principles; and (2) *Human-centered Evaluations of Explanations* at NAACL 2022[2], which contributes a taxonomy of human-centered evaluation of explanations. Both tutorials have some topical overlaps with our tutorial: data labeling is a particular form of interaction, crowdsourcing-based interaction will be covered in *Evaluate Model Us-*

[1] `https://nlp-crowdsourcing.github.io/`

[2] `https://xai-hcee.github.io/`

ability, and explanations presentation will be covered in *Interaction Design*. However, we believe the overlap is not substantial, as we only instruct these elements as "parameters" in human-model interaction. Instead, we hope our tutorial will be complementary to the previous ones.

Additionally, workshops like CHAI, NLP+HCI, and DADC (NAACL 2022) has gathered researchers in the field to explore the frontiers of relevant topics, whereas our tutorial will do a systematic reflection correspondingly.

3 Diversity Considerations

Our chosen tutorial topic inherently touches on *human user distribution*. As mentioned before, we will discuss the importance of high coverage of user groups, and the impact of design biases on people from different demographics (e.g., ages, cultures, languages, and gender). As such, we believe our tutorial will be a strong advocate for diversity in the NLP model and interaction designs.

Besides diversity-related topics, our presenter team will also make our tutorial more accessible to different user groups. Specifically, we will share our tutorial with a worldwide audience by promoting it on social media. we will also work with *CL D&I teams, and consult resources such as the BIG directory to diversify our audience participation.

4 Prerequisites & Reading List

The tutorial is targeted toward NLP researchers and practitioners working with humans. The prerequisite includes familiarity with basic knowledge of NLP and language systems. Knowledge of system deployment is a plus. We will also provide a more paced introduction to some materials.

The authors will also release an NLP+HCI playbook as a resource for people interested in getting started in human-centered NLP research. Here are a few papers that lay a foundation for this area:

- Putting Humans in the Natural Language Processing Loop: A Survey (Wang et al., 2021);
- All That's Human Is Not Gold: Evaluating Human Evaluation of Generated Text (Clark et al., 2021);
- Re-examining Whether, Why, and How Human-AI Interaction Is Uniquely Difficult to Design (Yang et al., 2020);
- Does the whole exceed its parts? The effect of AI explanations on complementary team performance (Wu & Bansal et al., 2021);
- Principles of mixed-initiative user interfaces (Horvitz, 1999);
- Guidelines for Human-AI Interaction (Amershi et al., 2019);
- Training language models to follow instructions with human feedback (Ouyang et al., 2022);
- Learning to summarize with human feedback (Stiennon et al., 2020)

5 Tutorial Presenters

Sherry Tongshuang Wu (she/her) is an assistant professor at the Human-Computer Interaction Institute, Carnegie Mellon University. Her primary research investigates how humans (AI experts, lay users, domain experts) interact with (debug, audit, and collaborate) AI systems. Sherry has organized two workshops at NLP and HCI conferences: Shared Stories and Lessons Learned workshop at EMNLP 2022 and Trust and Reliance in AI-Human Teams at CHI 2022. She is currently developing a new course on Human-Centered NLP at CMU.

Diyi Yang (she/her) is an assistant professor in the CS Department at Stanford University. Her research focuses on learning with limited and noisy text data, user-centric language generation, and computational social science. Diyi has organized four workshops at NLP conferences: Widening NLP Workshops at NAACL 2018 and ACL 2019, Casual Inference workshop at EMNLP 2021, and NLG Evaluation workshop at EMNLP 2021. She also gave a tutorial at the ACL 2022 on Learning with Limited Data. She has taught courses on natural language processing at Georgia Tech since 2019 and is now developing a new course on Human-Centered NLP at Stanford University.

Sebastin Santy (he/him) is a second-year PhD student at the Paul G. Allen School of CSE, University of Washington. He works on problems in the intersection of HCI and NLP and specifically his research focuses on uncovering design biases in NLP systems. He previously worked on multilinguality and machine translation.

6 Ethics Statement

We do not anticipate any ethical issues related to the tutorial logistics, but we plan to cover ethical considerations in our content, especially when we discuss human-centered evaluation metrics like safety, and when we review the impact of different communication and initiation methods in interaction designs (e.g. leading to confirmation biases).

References

Saleema Amershi, Dan Weld, Mihaela Vorvoreanu, Adam Fourney, Besmira Nushi, Penny Collisson, Jina Suh, Shamsi Iqbal, Paul N Bennett, Kori Inkpen, et al. 2019. Guidelines for human-ai interaction. In *Proceedings of the 2019 chi conference on human factors in computing systems*, pages 1–13.

Sandeep Avula, Bogeum Choi, and Jaime Arguello. 2022. The effects of system initiative during conversational collaborative search. *Proceedings of the ACM on Human-Computer Interaction*, 6(CSCW1):1–30.

Gagan Bansal, Besmira Nushi, Ece Kamar, Eric Horvitz, and Daniel S Weld. 2021. Is the most accurate ai the best teammate? optimizing ai for teamwork. In *Proceedings of the AAAI Conference on Artificial Intelligence*, volume 35, pages 11405–11414.

Shaily Bhatt, Rahul Jain, Sandipan Dandapat, and Sunayana Sitaram. 2021. A case study of efficacy and challenges in practical human-in-loop evaluation of nlp systems using checklist. In *Proceedings of the Workshop on Human Evaluation of NLP Systems (HumEval)*, pages 120–130.

Ángel Alexander Cabrera, Abraham J Druck, Jason I Hong, and Adam Perer. 2021. Discovering and validating ai errors with crowdsourced failure reports. *Proceedings of the ACM on Human-Computer Interaction*, 5(CSCW2):1–22.

Elizabeth Clark, Tal August, Sofia Serrano, Nikita Haduong, Suchin Gururangan, and Noah A Smith. 2021. All that's' human'is not gold: Evaluating human evaluation of generated text. *arXiv preprint arXiv:2107.00061*.

Hai Dang, Lukas Mecke, Florian Lehmann, Sven Goller, and Daniel Buschek. 2022. How to prompt? opportunities and challenges of zero-and few-shot learning for human-ai interaction in creative applications of generative models. *arXiv preprint arXiv:2209.01390*.

Sumanth Dathathri, Andrea Madotto, Janice Lan, Jane Hung, Eric Frank, Piero Molino, Jason Yosinski, and Rosanne Liu. 2019. Plug and play language models: A simple approach to controlled text generation. *arXiv preprint arXiv:1912.02164*.

Katy Ilonka Gero, Vivian Liu, and Lydia Chilton. 2022. Sparks: Inspiration for science writing using language models. In *Designing Interactive Systems Conference*, pages 1002–1019.

Ana Valeria Gonzalez, Gagan Bansal, Angela Fan, Robin Jia, Yashar Mehdad, and Srinivasan Iyer. 2020. Human evaluation of spoken vs. visual explanations for open-domain qa. *arXiv preprint arXiv:2012.15075*.

Spence Green, Jason Chuang, Jeffrey Heer, and Christopher D Manning. 2014a. Predictive translation memory: A mixed-initiative system for human language translation. In *Proceedings of the 27th annual ACM symposium on User interface software and technology*, pages 177–187.

Spence Green, Jeffrey Heer, and Christopher D Manning. 2013. The efficacy of human post-editing for language translation. In *Proceedings of the SIGCHI conference on human factors in computing systems*, pages 439–448.

Spence Green, Sida I Wang, Jason Chuang, Jeffrey Heer, Sebastian Schuster, and Christopher D Manning. 2014b. Human effort and machine learnability in computer aided translation. In *Proceedings of the 2014 Conference on Empirical Methods in Natural Language Processing (EMNLP)*, pages 1225–1236.

Eric Horvitz. 1999. Principles of mixed-initiative user interfaces. In *Proceedings of the SIGCHI conference on Human Factors in Computing Systems*, pages 159–166.

Ellen Jiang, Kristen Olson, Edwin Toh, Alejandra Molina, Aaron Donsbach, Michael Terry, and Carrie J Cai. 2022. Promptmaker: Prompt-based prototyping with large language models. In *CHI Conference on Human Factors in Computing Systems Extended Abstracts*, pages 1–8.

Pranav Khadpe, Ranjay Krishna, Li Fei-Fei, Jeffrey T Hancock, and Michael S Bernstein. 2020. Conceptual metaphors impact perceptions of human-ai collaboration. *Proceedings of the ACM on Human-Computer Interaction*, 4(CSCW2):1–26.

Hyunwoo Kim, Youngjae Yu, Liwei Jiang, Ximing Lu, Daniel Khashabi, Gunhee Kim, Yejin Choi, and Maarten Sap. 2022. Prosocialdialog: A prosocial backbone for conversational agents. *arXiv preprint arXiv:2205.12688*.

Ranjay Krishna, Donsuk Lee, Li Fei-Fei, and Michael S Bernstein. 2022. Socially situated artificial intelligence enables learning from human interaction. *Proceedings of the National Academy of Sciences*, 119(39):e2115730119.

Mike Kuniavsky. 2003. *Observing the user experience: a practitioner's guide to user research*. Elsevier.

Mina Lee, Percy Liang, and Qian Yang. 2022. Coauthor: Designing a human-ai collaborative writing dataset for exploring language model capabilities. In *CHI Conference on Human Factors in Computing Systems*, pages 1–19.

Huihan Li, Tianyu Gao, Manan Goenka, and Danqi Chen. 2021. Ditch the gold standard: Re-evaluating conversational question answering. *arXiv preprint arXiv:2112.08812*.

Changhoon Oh, Jungwoo Song, Jinhan Choi, Seonghyeon Kim, Sungwoo Lee, and Bongwon Suh. 2018. I lead, you help but only with enough details: Understanding user experience of co-creation with artificial intelligence. In *Proceedings of the 2018 CHI Conference on Human Factors in Computing Systems*, pages 1–13.

Dan R Olsen Jr. 2007. Evaluating user interface systems research. In *Proceedings of the 20th annual ACM symposium on User interface software and technology*, pages 251–258.

Long Ouyang, Jeff Wu, Xu Jiang, Diogo Almeida, Carroll L Wainwright, Pamela Mishkin, Chong Zhang, Sandhini Agarwal, Katarina Slama, Alex Ray, et al. 2022. Training language models to follow instructions with human feedback. *arXiv preprint arXiv:2203.02155*.

Joon Sung Park, Lindsay Popowski, Carrie Cai, Meredith Ringel Morris, Percy Liang, and Michael S Bernstein. 2022. Social simulacra: Creating populated prototypes for social computing systems. In *Proceedings of the 35th Annual ACM Symposium on User Interface Software and Technology*, pages 1–18.

Alexander J Ratner, Christopher M De Sa, Sen Wu, Daniel Selsam, and Christopher Ré. 2016. Data programming: Creating large training sets, quickly. *Advances in neural information processing systems*, 29.

Abhilasha Ravichander, Siddharth Dalmia, Maria Ryskina, Florian Metze, Eduard Hovy, and Alan W Black. 2021. NoiseQA: Challenge Set Evaluation for User-Centric Question Answering. In *Conference of the European Chapter of the Association for Computational Linguistics (EACL)*, Online.

Laria Reynolds and Kyle McDonell. 2021. Prompt programming for large language models: Beyond the few-shot paradigm. In *Extended Abstracts of the 2021 CHI Conference on Human Factors in Computing Systems*, pages 1–7.

Marco Tulio Ribeiro, Tongshuang Wu, Carlos Guestrin, and Sameer Singh. 2020. Beyond accuracy: Behavioral testing of nlp models with checklist. *arXiv preprint arXiv:2005.04118*.

S Roopa and MS Rani. 2012. Questionnaire designing for a survey. *Journal of Indian Orthodontic Society*, 46(4_suppl1):273–277.

Nithya Sambasivan, Shivani Kapania, Hannah Highfill, Diana Akrong, Praveen Paritosh, and Lora M Aroyo. 2021. "everyone wants to do the model work, not the data work": Data cascades in high-stakes ai. In *proceedings of the 2021 CHI Conference on Human Factors in Computing Systems*, pages 1–15.

Sebastin Santy, Kalika Bali, Monojit Choudhury, Sandipan Dandapat, Tanuja Ganu, Anurag Shukla, Jahanvi Shah, and Vivek Seshadri. 2021. Language translation as a socio-technical system: Case-studies of mixed-initiative interactions. In *ACM SIGCAS Conference on Computing and Sustainable Societies*, pages 156–172.

Sebastin Santy, Sandipan Dandapat, Monojit Choudhury, and Kalika Bali. 2019. Inmt: Interactive neural machine translation prediction. In *Proceedings of the 2019 Conference on Empirical Methods in Natural Language Processing and the 9th International Joint Conference on Natural Language Processing (EMNLP-IJCNLP): System Demonstrations*, pages 103–108.

Nisan Stiennon, Long Ouyang, Jeffrey Wu, Daniel Ziegler, Ryan Lowe, Chelsea Voss, Alec Radford, Dario Amodei, and Paul F Christiano. 2020. Learning to summarize with human feedback. *Advances in Neural Information Processing Systems*, 33:3008–3021.

Romal Thoppilan, Daniel De Freitas, Jamie Hall, Noam Shazeer, Apoorv Kulshreshtha, Heng-Tze Cheng, Alicia Jin, Taylor Bos, Leslie Baker, Yu Du, et al. 2022. Lamda: Language models for dialog applications. *arXiv preprint arXiv:2201.08239*.

Eric Wallace, Pedro Rodriguez, Shi Feng, Ikuya Yamada, and Jordan Boyd-Graber. 2019. Trick me if you can: Human-in-the-loop generation of adversarial examples for question answering. *Transactions of the Association for Computational Linguistics*, 7:387–401.

Yun Wang, Zhitao Hou, Leixian Shen, Tongshuang Wu, Jiaqi Wang, He Huang, Haidong Zhang, and Dongmei Zhang. 2022. Towards natural language-based visualization authoring. *IEEE Transactions on Visualization and Computer Graphics*.

Zijie J Wang, Dongjin Choi, Shenyu Xu, and Diyi Yang. 2021. Putting humans in the natural language processing loop: A survey. *arXiv preprint arXiv:2103.04044*.

Tongshuang & Gagan Wu & Bansal, Joyce Zhou, Raymond Fok, Besmira Nushi, Ece Kamar, Marco Tulio Ribeiro, and Daniel Weld. 2021. Does the whole exceed its parts? the effect of ai explanations on complementary team performance. In *Proceedings of the 2021 CHI Conference on Human Factors in Computing Systems*, pages 1–16.

Tongshuang Wu, Michael Terry, and Carrie Jun Cai. 2022. Ai chains: Transparent and controllable human-ai interaction by chaining large language model prompts. In *CHI Conference on Human Factors in Computing Systems*, pages 1–22.

Qian Yang, Aaron Steinfeld, Carolyn Rosé, and John Zimmerman. 2020. Re-examining whether, why, and how human-ai interaction is uniquely difficult to design. In *Proceedings of the 2020 chi conference on human factors in computing systems*, pages 1–13.

LLM-driven Instruction Following: Progresses and Concerns

Wenpeng Yin[†], **Qinyuan Ye**[‡], **Pengfei Liu**[◇], **Xiang Ren**[‡] and **Hinrich Schütze**[♯]
[†]Penn State; [‡]USC; [◇]SJTU; [♯]LMU Munich
wenpeng@psu.edu; {qinyuany, xiangren}@usc.edu
stefanpengfei@gmail.com; hinrich@hotmail.com

Abstract

The progress of natural language processing (NLP) is primarily driven by machine learning that optimizes a system on a large-scale set of task-specific labeled examples. This learning paradigm limits the ability of machines to have the same capabilities as humans in handling new tasks since humans can often solve unseen tasks with a couple of examples accompanied by task instructions. In addition, we may not have a chance to prepare task-specific examples of large-volume for new tasks because we cannot foresee what task needs to be addressed next and how complex to annotate for it. Therefore, task instructions act as a novel and promising resource for supervision.

This tutorial targets researchers and practitioners who are interested in AI and ML technologies for NLP generalization in a low-shot scenario. In particular, we will present a diverse thread of instruction-driven NLP studies that try to answer the following questions: (i) What is task instruction? (ii) How is the process of creating datasets and evaluating systems conducted? (iii) How to encode task instructions? (iv) When and why do some instructions work better? (v) What concerns remain in LLM-driven instruction following? We will discuss several lines of frontier research that tackle those challenges and will conclude the tutorial by outlining directions for further investigation.

1 Introduction

This proposal is driven by a fundamental question of task generalization in NLP: how to comprehend a new task if labeled examples are pretty limited? One goal of AI is to build a system that can continually understand and solve new tasks. Labeled examples, as the mainstream task representation, are unlikely to be available in large numbers or even do not exist. Then, is there any other task representation that can contribute to task comprehension? Task instructions provide another dimension of supervision for expressing the task semantics. Instructions often contain more abstract and comprehensive knowledge of the target task than individual labeled examples. With the availability of task instructions, systems can be quickly built to handle new tasks, especially when task-specific annotations are scarce (Wang et al., 2022; Yin et al., 2022). Instruction following is inspired by the typical human learning for new tasks, e.g., a little kid can well solve a new mathematical task by learning from its instruction and a few examples. This new learning paradigm has recently begun to attract the attention of the machine learning and NLP communities.

Despite the importance, frontier research in instruction following is still struggling with the following questions. First, should instructions be constructed to express the target task as detailed as possible (e.g., MTurk instructions (Mishra et al., 2022)) or to align with the format of supervising tasks (e.g., natural language inference (Yin et al., 2019) or language modeling (Brown et al., 2020)) as well as possible? Second, how to effectively encode instructions that may consist of some specific requirements such as "maximal output length 5", and "do not generate anything else apart from one of the following ···"? Third, what are the factors (e.g., model size, task numbers) that influence a system's generalization, robustness, etc.? Fourth, how to evaluate instruction-following systems? Last, what is the future for academia and industry in this ChatGPT era?

In this tutorial, we will systematically review several lines of frontier research on developing systems that are supervised by task instructions. Beyond introducing pioneering work that parsed instructions to cope with individual tasks, such as soccer game (Kuhlmann et al., 2004), software control (Branavan et al., 2009, 2011), etc., we will focus on recent LLM-based approaches for cross-task generalization given task instructions. Specifically, in light of the heterogeneous formats and dis-

Proceedings of the 2023 Conference on Empirical Methods in Natural Language Processing: Tutorial Abstracts, pages 19–25
December 6-10, 2023 ©2023 Association for Computational Linguistics

parate rationales underlying instructions, we shall endeavor to establish a unified lens for interpreting the essence of various instructions. Subsequently, a structured exposition and critical analysis will be undertaken, encompassing a spectrum of aspects such as diverse instruction-following datasets, rigorous evaluation methodologies, multifaceted performance-influencing factors, and lingering concerns within this domain.

Participants will learn about recent trends and emerging challenges in this topic, representative tools and learning resources to obtain ready-to-use models, and how related technologies benefit end-user NLP applications.

2 Outline of Tutorial Content

This **half-day** tutorial presents a systematic overview of recent advancements in NLP with supervision from task instructions. The detailed contents are outlined below.

2.1 Background and motivation [20min]

We will define the main research problem and motivate the topic by presenting several real-world NLP and instruction-driven AI applications, as well as several key challenges that are at the core of classic machine learning.

2.2 What is the essence of instructions? [30min]

Various researchers may hold differing viewpoints on the nature of instructions, with some specializing in particular types of instructions while overlooking the interconnections among various instruction categories. In this section, we aim to establish a unified perspective for understanding the essence of instructions.

We begin by introducing various typical forms of instructions. For instance, some instructions serve to elucidate the output labels in classification tasks, as exemplified by **NLI-oriented task instructions** (Yin et al., 2019; Xu et al., 2022; Li et al., 2022; Xia et al., 2021; Sainz et al., 2021, 2022). These instructions treat the outputs as hypotheses and transform the target problems into natural language inference (NLI) to leverage the supervision available in existing NLI datasets. Other instructions aim to enhance the input text, such as prompts, which are designed to leverage the rich supervision from pretrained language models (Radford et al., 2019; Schick and Schütze, 2021b,a, 2022). Thus, they are referred to as **LM-oriented instructions**. Additionally, there are more natural instructions contributed by end-users who lack expertise in machine learning or LLMs. These instructions attempt to convey the task's semantics regardless of the specific technique to be employed. We categorize these as **human-oriented instructions** (Efrat and Levy, 2020; Mishra et al., 2022; Wang et al., 2022; Lou et al., 2023). To adhere to human-oriented instructions, LLMs are frequently trained on a diverse array of instruction-following tasks. Consequently, we consolidate these distinct types of instructions under the umbrella term *instructions as supervision-oriented textual expressions*.

2.3 Instruction-following datasets and evaluations [30min]

Initially, we introduce a range of **crowdsourced datasets**, which include P3 (Sanh et al.), Big-bench (Srivastava et al., 2022), Dolly (Conover et al., 2023), Natural-Instructions (Mishra et al., 2022; Wang et al., 2022), Multi-Instruct (Xu et al., 2023b), etc. Nevertheless, human-crafted datasets have inherent limitations due to the constraints of human effort, making it challenging to expand the diversity and complexity of tasks. Consequently, recent efforts have turned to **LLM-generated datasets**, as exemplified by Self-Instruct (Wang et al., 2023), Unnatural-Instruct (Honovich et al., 2023), Dynosaur (Yin et al., 2023), WizardLM (Xu et al., 2023a), LongForm (Köksal et al., 2023), Muffin (Lou et al., 2023), and others. Irrespective of the datasets' origin, this tutorial will elucidate their objectives and distinctions from a scaling perspective.

Regarding the evaluation, we commence with automated assessments conducted on a selection of high-quality crowdsourced datasets, including Natural-Instructions (Mishra et al., 2022; Wang et al., 2022), T0 (Sanh et al.), Big-bench (Srivastava et al., 2022), etc. Subsequently, we introduce Vicuna system (Chiang et al., 2023), which employed GPT-4[1] for automated evaluations. Finally, we proceed to human assessments, which take into account various criteria, as demonstrated in works such as (Wang et al., 2023; Yin et al., 2023; Askell et al., 2021).

[1]https://openai.com/research/gpt-4

2.4 Methodology for instruction tuning [30min]

An established experimental framework for instruction tuning entails initially training a model on a set of provided instructions and subsequently assessing its performance on unseen instructions. In this context, we will present three distinct methodologies for modeling instructions: (i) The **Concatenation** method, which involves the straightforward concatenation of elements from the instruction and task input to form a lengthy textual sequence. This composite sequence is then fed into an LLM to generate the desired output. Representative works include (Mishra et al., 2022; Wang et al., 2022; Yin et al., 2022). (ii) **Hypernetwork-based approaches** (Ye and Ren, 2021; Ivison et al., 2022), where a hypernetwork (Ha et al., 2017) is trained to generate instruction-specific model parameters, which are subsequently integrated into a primary network. (iii) **Reinforcement learning with human feedback** methods (Bai et al., 2022; Ouyang et al., 2022; Stiennon et al., 2020), which involve the utilization of reinforcement learning techniques guided by human-provided comparison data.

2.5 When and why it works [30min]

Most instruction-driven systems assume that each task has a single instruction. We can imagine that different users can convey a task with instructions of distinct textual expressions. Some prompt-based LLMs also show varying performance in dealing with prompts of different templates (Schick and Schütze, 2022; Kojima et al., 2022). A question arises: how to predict and explain an instruction' behavior? To the end, we first introduce the work by Gu et al. (2023) that explored the robustness of pretrained instruction learning system in handling (i) the same task with distinct instructions written by different MTurkers, and (ii) instruction of varying degrees of abstractions. Then, we present a series of works that i) explain prompts performance by LLM-oriented perplexity (Gonen et al., 2022), the model bias (Zhao et al., 2021), or ii) improve instructions by reformulating them into more effective ones (Khashabi et al., 2022).

2.6 Concerns of instruction following [30min]

In this section, we will address concerns related to instruction following across four distinct dimensions: (i) The "inverse scaling law" observed in LLMs when dealing with negation (Mishra et al., 2022; Jang et al., 2022; Hossain et al., 2022). (ii) Unanticipated behavior arising in the realm of instruction comprehension, drawing from human capabilities in following instructions (Webson and Pavlick, 2022). (iii) The issue of task-hungry models. Despite shifting our research focus from cross-example generalization to cross-task generation, the creation of large-scale instruction-following datasets presents another challenge. To enhance LLMs' instruction-following abilities for new tasks, the collection of extensive training tasks becomes a necessity. (iv) The emergence of adversarial instruction attacks (Shu et al., 2023; Wan et al., 2023; Kang et al., 2023; Li et al., 2023).

2.7 Future directions [10min]

In the last section, we will discuss some critical and foreshadowing research directions, such as scalable oversight and alignment (Hendrycks et al., 2021; Bowman et al., 2022), explainable instruction learning, and how to encode instructions without the help of labeled examples, etc.

3 Specification of the Tutorial

The proposed tutorial is considered a **cutting-edge** tutorial that introduces new frontiers in instruction-driven NLP. The presented topic has not been covered by any ACL/EMNLP/EACL/NAACL/AACL/COLING tutorials in the past 4 years. A tiny overlap exists between our section "LM-oriented task instructions" and the ACL tutorial (Beltagy et al., 2022), which presented LLM techniques for NLP. But Beltagy et al. (2022) focused on various training techniques, such as self-training, meta-training, etc., our tutorial has a broader scope of instruction learning, in which prompt-based LLM is merely a sub-area.

Audience and Prerequisites Based on the level of interest in this topic, we expect around 150 participants. While no specific background knowledge is assumed of the audience, it would be best for the attendees to know about basic deep learning technologies, pre-trained language models (e.g., BERT). A **reading list** that could help provide background knowledge to the audience before attending this tutorial is given in Appendix A.1.

Breadth We estimate that at least 60% of the work covered in this tutorial is from researchers other than the instructors of the tutorial.

Diversity Considerations This tutorial will cover instruction learning for NLP as well as non-NLP problems, such as instruction-driven navigation, software control, etc. We will also cover content applying instruction supervision for individual tasks as well as cross-task generation. Our presenter team has a diverse background regarding geography and gender. Our team will promote our tutorial on social media to diversify our audience participation.

Material Access Online All the materials are openly available at `www.wenpengyin.org/publications`

4 Tutorial Instructors

The following are biographies of the speaker.

Wenpeng Yin is an Assistant Professor in the Department of Computer Science and Engineering at Penn State University. His research focuses on NLP with three sub-areas: (i) learning from task instructions; (ii) information extraction; (iii) NLP for education, bioinformatics, etc. Dr. Yin has presented the tutorial "Indirectly Supervised Natural Language Processing" at ACL'23, and tutorial "Learning from Task Instructions" at KONVENS'23. Additional information is available at `www.wenpengyin.org`.

Qinyuan Ye is a fifth-year Ph.D. student at the University of Southern California, advised by Prof. Xiang Ren. Her research interest lies in natural language processing. In particular she is interested in approaches that reduce human annotation efforts, including methods leveraging distant supervision, high-level human supervision (e.g., explanations, instructions), and meta-learning. Additional information is available at `yeqy.xyz`.

Pengfei Liu is an associate professor at Shanghai Jiaotong University and leads the Generative Artificial Intelligence Research Lab (GAIR). His research topics currently focus on information extraction, text generation, language pre-training, and NLP system evaluation. He won the Best Demo Paper award in ACL 2021 and the Outstanding Demo Paper award in ACL 2022. Homepage: `http://pfliu.com`.

Xiang Ren is an Associate Professor in Computer Science and the Andrew and Erna Viterbi Early Career Chair at USC. Ren's research seeks to build generalizable NLP systems that can handle a wide variety of language tasks and situations. He works on new algorithms and datasets to make NLP systems cheaper to develop and maintain, arm machine models with common sense, and improve model's transparency and reliability to build user trust. His research work has received several best paper awards in top NLP and AI conference venues. Ren has been awarded an NSF CAREER Award, multiple faculty research awards from Google, Facebook, Amazon, JP Morgan and Sony, and the 2018 ACM SIGKDD Doctoral Dissertation Award. He was named Forbes' Asia 30 Under 30 in 2019. Ren has presented a number of tutorials, such as Knowledge-Augmented Methods for Natural Language Processing at ACL 2022, Scalable Construction and Reasoning of Massive Knowledge Bases at NAACL 2018, and other related tutorials at WWW'18, CIKM'17, etc. Homepage: `https://shanzhenren.github.io`.

Hinrich Schütze is Chair of Computational Linguistics and co-director of the Center of Information and Language Processing at Ludwig-Maximilians-Universität München (LMU Munich), Germany. He was the President of the Association for Computational Linguistics in 2020, and General Chair of ACL 2013. In 2022, Prof. Schütze was elected as ACL Fellow. Prior to joining LMU Munich, he was a Professor of Theoretical Computational Linguistics at the University of Stuttgart. Hinrich holds a Ph.D. in computational linguistics from Stanford University. Additional information is available at `https://schuetze.cis.lmu.de`.

Ethical Considerations

We do not anticipate any ethical issues particularly to the topics of the tutorial.

References

Amanda Askell, Yuntao Bai, Anna Chen, Dawn Drain, Deep Ganguli, Tom Henighan, Andy Jones, Nicholas Joseph, Benjamin Mann, Nova DasSarma, Nelson Elhage, Zac Hatfield-Dodds, Danny Hernandez, Jackson Kernion, Kamal Ndousse, Catherine Olsson, Dario Amodei, Tom B. Brown, Jack Clark, Sam McCandlish, Chris Olah, and Jared Kaplan. 2021. A general language assistant as a laboratory for alignment. *CoRR*, abs/2112.00861.

Yuntao Bai, Andy Jones, Kamal Ndousse, Amanda Askell, Anna Chen, Nova DasSarma, Dawn Drain,

Stanislav Fort, Deep Ganguli, Tom Henighan, Nicholas Joseph, Saurav Kadavath, Jackson Kernion, Tom Conerly, Sheer El Showk, Nelson Elhage, Zac Hatfield-Dodds, Danny Hernandez, Tristan Hume, Scott Johnston, Shauna Kravec, Liane Lovitt, Neel Nanda, Catherine Olsson, Dario Amodei, Tom B. Brown, Jack Clark, Sam McCandlish, Chris Olah, Benjamin Mann, and Jared Kaplan. 2022. Training a helpful and harmless assistant with reinforcement learning from human feedback. *CoRR*, abs/2204.05862.

Iz Beltagy, Arman Cohan, Robert Logan IV, Sewon Min, and Sameer Singh. 2022. Zero- and few-shot NLP with pretrained language models. In *Proceedings of the 60th Annual Meeting of the Association for Computational Linguistics: Tutorial Abstracts*, pages 32–37, Dublin, Ireland. Association for Computational Linguistics.

Samuel R Bowman, Jeeyoon Hyun, Ethan Perez, Edwin Chen, Craig Pettit, Scott Heiner, Kamile Lukosuite, Amanda Askell, Andy Jones, Anna Chen, et al. 2022. Measuring progress on scalable oversight for large language models. *arXiv preprint arXiv:2211.03540*.

S. R. K. Branavan, Harr Chen, Luke Zettlemoyer, and Regina Barzilay. 2009. Reinforcement learning for mapping instructions to actions. In *Proceedings of ACL*, pages 82–90.

S. R. K. Branavan, David Silver, and Regina Barzilay. 2011. Learning to win by reading manuals in a monte-carlo framework. In *Proceedings of ACL*, pages 268–277.

Tom B. Brown, Benjamin Mann, Nick Ryder, Melanie Subbiah, Jared Kaplan, Prafulla Dhariwal, Arvind Neelakantan, Pranav Shyam, Girish Sastry, Amanda Askell, Sandhini Agarwal, Ariel Herbert-Voss, Gretchen Krueger, Tom Henighan, Rewon Child, Aditya Ramesh, Daniel M. Ziegler, Jeffrey Wu, Clemens Winter, Christopher Hesse, Mark Chen, Eric Sigler, Mateusz Litwin, Scott Gray, Benjamin Chess, Jack Clark, Christopher Berner, Sam McCandlish, Alec Radford, Ilya Sutskever, and Dario Amodei. 2020. Language models are few-shot learners. In *Advances in Neural Information Processing Systems 33: Annual Conference on Neural Information Processing Systems 2020, NeurIPS 2020, December 6-12, 2020, virtual*.

Wei-Lin Chiang, Zhuohan Li, Zi Lin, Ying Sheng, Zhanghao Wu, Hao Zhang, Lianmin Zheng, Siyuan Zhuang, Yonghao Zhuang, Joseph E. Gonzalez, Ion Stoica, and Eric P. Xing. 2023. Vicuna: An open-source chatbot impressing gpt-4 with 90%* chatgpt quality.

Mike Conover, Matt Hayes, Ankit Mathur, Jianwei Xie, Jun Wan, Sam Shah, Ali Ghodsi, Patrick Wendell, Matei Zaharia, and Reynold Xin. 2023. Free dolly: Introducing the world's first truly open instruction-tuned llm.

Avia Efrat and Omer Levy. 2020. The turking test: Can language models understand instructions? *CoRR*, abs/2010.11982.

Dan Goldwasser and Dan Roth. 2011. Learning from natural instructions. In *IJCAI 2011, Proceedings of the 22nd International Joint Conference on Artificial Intelligence, Barcelona, Catalonia, Spain, July 16-22, 2011*, pages 1794–1800. IJCAI/AAAI.

Hila Gonen, Srini Iyer, Terra Blevins, Noah A. Smith, and Luke Zettlemoyer. 2022. Demystifying prompts in language models via perplexity estimation. *CoRR*, abs/2212.04037.

Jiasheng Gu, Hongyu Zhao, Hanzi Xu, Liangyu Nie, Hongyuan Mei, and Wenpeng Yin. 2023. Robustness of learning from task instructions. In *Findings of ACL*, pages 13935–13948.

David Ha, Andrew M. Dai, and Quoc V. Le. 2017. Hypernetworks. In *ICLR*.

Dan Hendrycks, Collin Burns, Steven Basart, Andrew Critch, Jerry Li, Dawn Song, and Jacob Steinhardt. 2021. Aligning AI with shared human values. In *ICLR*.

Or Honovich, Thomas Scialom, Omer Levy, and Timo Schick. 2023. Unnatural instructions: Tuning language models with (almost) no human labor. In *Proceedings of ACL*, pages 14409–14428.

Md Mosharaf Hossain, Dhivya Chinnappa, and Eduardo Blanco. 2022. An analysis of negation in natural language understanding corpora. In *Proceedings of ACL*, pages 716–723.

Hamish Ivison, Akshita Bhagia, Yizhong Wang, Hannaneh Hajishirzi, and Matthew Peters. 2022. Hint: Hypernetwork instruction tuning for efficient zero-shot generalisation. *arXiv preprint arXiv:2212.10315*.

Joel Jang, Seonghyeon Ye, and Minjoon Seo. 2022. Can large language models truly understand prompts? A case study with negated prompts. In *Transfer Learning for Natural Language Processing Workshop, 03 December 2022, New Orleans, Louisiana, USA*, volume 203 of *Proceedings of Machine Learning Research*, pages 52–62. PMLR.

Daniel Kang, Xuechen Li, Ion Stoica, Carlos Guestrin, Matei Zaharia, and Tatsunori Hashimoto. 2023. Exploiting programmatic behavior of llms: Dual-use through standard security attacks. *CoRR*, abs/2302.05733.

Daniel Khashabi, Chitta Baral, Yejin Choi, and Hannaneh Hajishirzi. 2022. Reframing instructional prompts to gptk's language. In *Findings of ACL*, pages 589–612.

Takeshi Kojima, Shixiang Shane Gu, Machel Reid, Yutaka Matsuo, and Yusuke Iwasawa. 2022. Large language models are zero-shot reasoners. In *NeurIPS*.

Abdullatif Köksal, Timo Schick, Anna Korhonen, and Hinrich Schütze. 2023. Longform: Optimizing instruction tuning for long text generation with corpus extraction. *CoRR*, abs/2304.08460.

Gregory Kuhlmann, Peter Stone, Raymond Mooney, and Jude Shavlik. 2004. Guiding a reinforcement learner with natural language advice: Initial results in robocup soccer. In *The AAAI workshop on supervisory control of learning and adaptive systems*, pages 30–35.

Bangzheng Li, Wenpeng Yin, and Muhao Chen. 2022. Ultra-fine entity typing with indirect supervision from natural language inference. *Trans. Assoc. Comput. Linguistics*, 10:607–622.

Zekun Li, Baolin Peng, Pengcheng He, and Xifeng Yan. 2023. Do you really follow me? adversarial instructions for evaluating the robustness of large language models. *CoRR*, abs/2308.10819.

Pengfei Liu, Weizhe Yuan, Jinlan Fu, Zhengbao Jiang, Hiroaki Hayashi, and Graham Neubig. 2021. Pre-train, prompt, and predict: A systematic survey of prompting methods in natural language processing. *CoRR*, abs/2107.13586.

Renze Lou, Kai Zhang, Jian Xie, Yuxuan Sun, Janice Ahn, Hanzi Xu, Yu Su, and Wenpeng Yin. 2023. MUFFIN: Curating multi-faceted instructions for improving instruction following.

Swaroop Mishra, Daniel Khashabi, Chitta Baral, and Hannaneh Hajishirzi. 2022. Cross-task generalization via natural language crowdsourcing instructions. In *Proceedings of ACL*, pages 3470–3487.

Long Ouyang, Jeffrey Wu, Xu Jiang, Diogo Almeida, Carroll L. Wainwright, Pamela Mishkin, Chong Zhang, Sandhini Agarwal, Katarina Slama, Alex Ray, John Schulman, Jacob Hilton, Fraser Kelton, Luke Miller, Maddie Simens, Amanda Askell, Peter Welinder, Paul F. Christiano, Jan Leike, and Ryan Lowe. 2022. Training language models to follow instructions with human feedback. In *NeurIPS*.

Alec Radford, Jeffrey Wu, Rewon Child, David Luan, Dario Amodei, and Ilya Sutskever. 2019. Language models are unsupervised multitask learners. *OpenAI blog*.

Oscar Sainz, Oier Lopez de Lacalle, Gorka Labaka, Ander Barrena, and Eneko Agirre. 2021. Label verbalization and entailment for effective zero and few-shot relation extraction. In *Proceedings of EMNLP*, pages 1199–1212.

Oscar Sainz, Itziar Gonzalez-Dios, Oier Lopez de Lacalle, Bonan Min, and Eneko Agirre. 2022. Textual entailment for event argument extraction: Zero- and few-shot with multi-source learning. In *Findings of NAACL*, pages 2439–2455.

Victor Sanh, Albert Webson, Colin Raffel, Stephen H. Bach, Lintang Sutawika, Zaid Alyafeai, Antoine Chaffin, Arnaud Stiegler, Arun Raja, Manan Dey, M Saiful Bari, Canwen Xu, Urmish Thakker, Shanya Sharma Sharma, Eliza Szczechla, Taewoon Kim, Gunjan Chhablani, Nihal V. Nayak, Debajyoti Datta, Jonathan Chang, Mike Tian-Jian Jiang, Han Wang, Matteo Manica, Sheng Shen, Zheng Xin Yong, Harshit Pandey, Rachel Bawden, Thomas Wang, Trishala Neeraj, Jos Rozen, Abheesht Sharma, Andrea Santilli, Thibault Févry, Jason Alan Fries, Ryan Teehan, Teven Le Scao, Stella Biderman, Leo Gao, Thomas Wolf, and Alexander M. Rush. Multitask prompted training enables zero-shot task generalization. In *ICLR*.

Timo Schick and Hinrich Schütze. 2021a. Exploiting cloze-questions for few-shot text classification and natural language inference. In *Proceedings of EACL*, pages 255–269.

Timo Schick and Hinrich Schütze. 2021b. Few-shot text generation with natural language instructions. In *Proceedings of EMNLP*, pages 390–402.

Timo Schick and Hinrich Schütze. 2022. True few-shot learning with prompts - A real-world perspective. *Trans. Assoc. Comput. Linguistics*, 10:716–731.

Manli Shu, Jiongxiao Wang, Chen Zhu, Jonas Geiping, Chaowei Xiao, and Tom Goldstein. 2023. On the exploitability of instruction tuning. *CoRR*, abs/2306.17194.

Aarohi Srivastava, Abhinav Rastogi, Abhishek Rao, Abu Awal Md Shoeb, Abubakar Abid, Adam Fisch, Adam R. Brown, Adam Santoro, Aditya Gupta, Adrià Garriga-Alonso, Agnieszka Kluska, Aitor Lewkowycz, Akshat Agarwal, Alethea Power, Alex Ray, Alex Warstadt, Alexander W. Kocurek, Ali Safaya, Ali Tazarv, Alice Xiang, Alicia Parrish, Allen Nie, Aman Hussain, Amanda Askell, Amanda Dsouza, Ameet Rahane, Anantharaman S. Iyer, Anders Andreassen, Andrea Santilli, Andreas Stuhlmüller, Andrew M. Dai, Andrew La, Andrew K. Lampinen, Andy Zou, Angela Jiang, Angelica Chen, Anh Vuong, Animesh Gupta, Anna Gottardi, Antonio Norelli, Anu Venkatesh, Arash Gholamidavoodi, Arfa Tabassum, Arul Menezes, Arun Kirubarajan, Asher Mullokandov, Ashish Sabharwal, Austin Herrick, Avia Efrat, Aykut Erdem, Ayla Karakas, and et al. 2022. Beyond the imitation game: Quantifying and extrapolating the capabilities of language models. *CoRR*, abs/2206.04615.

Nisan Stiennon, Long Ouyang, Jeff Wu, Daniel M. Ziegler, Ryan Lowe, Chelsea Voss, Alec Radford, Dario Amodei, and Paul F. Christiano. 2020. Learning to summarize from human feedback. In *NeurIPS*.

Alexander Wan, Eric Wallace, Sheng Shen, and Dan Klein. 2023. Poisoning language models during instruction tuning. In *Proceedings of ICML*, volume 202, pages 35413–35425.

Yizhong Wang, Yeganeh Kordi, Swaroop Mishra, Alisa Liu, Noah A. Smith, Daniel Khashabi, and Hannaneh Hajishirzi. 2023. Self-instruct: Aligning language models with self-generated instructions. In *Proceedings of ACL*, pages 13484–13508.

Yizhong Wang, Swaroop Mishra, Pegah Alipoormolabashi, Yeganeh Kordi, Amirreza Mirzaei, Atharva Naik, Arjun Ashok, Arut Selvan Dhanasekaran, Anjana Arunkumar, David Stap, Eshaan Pathak, Giannis Karamanolakis, Haizhi Gary Lai, Ishan Purohit, Ishani Mondal, Jacob Anderson, Kirby Kuznia, Krima Doshi, Kuntal Kumar Pal, Maitreya Patel, Mehrad Moradshahi, Mihir Parmar, Mirali Purohit, Neeraj Varshney, Phani Rohitha Kaza, Pulkit Verma, Ravsehaj Singh Puri, Rushang Karia, Savan Doshi, Shailaja Keyur Sampat, Siddhartha Mishra, Sujan Reddy A, Sumanta Patro, Tanay Dixit, and Xudong Shen. 2022. Super-naturalinstructions: Generalization via declarative instructions on 1600+ NLP tasks. In *Proceedings of EMNLP*, pages 5085–5109.

Ziqi Wang, Yujia Qin, Wenxuan Zhou, Jun Yan, Qinyuan Ye, Leonardo Neves, Zhiyuan Liu, and Xiang Ren. 2020. Learning from explanations with neural execution tree. In *Proceedings of ICLR*.

Albert Webson and Ellie Pavlick. 2022. Do prompt-based models really understand the meaning of their prompts? In *Proceedings of NAACL*, pages 2300–2344.

Congying Xia, Wenpeng Yin, Yihao Feng, and Philip S. Yu. 2021. Incremental few-shot text classification with multi-round new classes: Formulation, dataset and system. In *Proceedings of NAACL-HLT*, pages 1351–1360.

Can Xu, Qingfeng Sun, Kai Zheng, Xiubo Geng, Pu Zhao, Jiazhan Feng, Chongyang Tao, and Daxin Jiang. 2023a. Wizardlm: Empowering large language models to follow complex instructions. *CoRR*, abs/2304.12244.

Hanzi Xu, Slobodan Vucetic, and Wenpeng Yin. 2022. Openstance: Real-world zero-shot stance detection. In *Proceedings of CoNLL*.

Zhiyang Xu, Ying Shen, and Lifu Huang. 2023b. Multiinstruct: Improving multi-modal zero-shot learning via instruction tuning. In *Proceedings of ACL*, pages 11445–11465.

Qinyuan Ye and Xiang Ren. 2021. Learning to generate task-specific adapters from task description. In *Proceedings of ACL/IJCNLP (Volume 2: Short Papers)*, pages 646–653.

Da Yin, Xiao Liu, Fan Yin, Ming Zhong, Hritik Bansal, Jiawei Han, and Kai-Wei Chang. 2023. Dynosaur: A dynamic growth paradigm for instruction-tuning data curation. *CoRR*, abs/2305.14327.

Wenpeng Yin, Jamaal Hay, and Dan Roth. 2019. Benchmarking zero-shot text classification: Datasets, evaluation and entailment approach. In *Proceedings of EMNLP-IJCNLP*, pages 3912–3921.

Wenpeng Yin, Jia Li, and Caiming Xiong. 2022. ConTinTin: Continual learning from task instructions. In *Proceedings of ACL*, pages 3062–3072.

Yichi Zhang and Joyce Chai. 2021. Hierarchical task learning from language instructions with unified transformers and self-monitoring. In *Findings of ACL/IJCNLP*, pages 4202–4213.

Zihao Zhao, Eric Wallace, Shi Feng, Dan Klein, and Sameer Singh. 2021. Calibrate before use: Improving few-shot performance of language models. In *Proceedings of ICML*, volume 139, pages 12697–12706.

A Appendix

A.1 Recommended Paper List

The following is a reading list that could help provide background knowledge to the audience before attending this tutorial:

- Learning from Natural Instructions (Goldwasser and Roth, 2011)
- Learning from Explanations with Neural Execution Tree (Wang et al., 2020)
- Benchmarking Zero-shot Text Classification: Datasets, Evaluation and Entailment Approach (Yin et al., 2019)
- Textual Entailment for Event Argument Extraction: Zero- and Few-Shot with Multi-Source Learning (Sainz et al., 2022)
- Pre-train, Prompt, and Predict: A Systematic Survey of Prompting Methods in Natural Language Processing (Liu et al., 2021)
- True Few-Shot Learning With Prompts—A Real-World Perspective (Schick and Schütze, 2022)
- The Turking Test: Can Language Models Understand Instructions? (Efrat and Levy, 2020)
- Hierarchical Task Learning from Language Instructions with Unified Transformers and Self-Monitoring (Zhang and Chai, 2021)
- Cross-Task Generalization via Natural Language Crowdsourcing Instructions (Mishra et al., 2022)
- MUFFIN: Curating Multi-Faceted Instructions for Improving Instruction Following (Lou et al., 2023)

Mitigating Societal Harms in Large Language Models

Sachin Kumar[*,♣] **Vidhisha Balachandran**[*,♣] **Lucille Njoo**[♡]
Antonios Anastasopoulos[◇] **Yulia Tsvetkov**[♡]
[♣]Language Technologies Institute, Carnegie Mellon University
[◇]Department of Computer Science, George Mason University
[♡]Paul G. Allen School of Computer Science & Engineering, University of Washington
{sachink,vbalacha}@cs.cmu.edu, lnjoo@cs.washington.edu
antonis@gmu.edu, yuliats@cs.washington.edu

Abstract

Numerous recent studies have highlighted societal harms that can be caused by language technologies deployed in the wild. While several surveys, tutorials, and workshops have discussed the risks of harms in specific contexts—e.g., detecting and mitigating gender bias in NLP models—no prior work has developed a unified typology of technical approaches for mitigating harms of language generation models. Our tutorial is based on a survey we recently wrote that proposes such a typology. We will provide an overview of potential social issues in language generation, including toxicity, social biases, misinformation, factual inconsistency, and privacy violations. Our primary focus will be on how to systematically identify risks, and how eliminate them at various stages of model development, from data collection, to model development, to inference/language generation. Through this tutorial, we aim to equip NLP researchers and engineers with a suite of practical tools for mitigating safety risks from pretrained language generation models.

1 Motivation

With the widespread success and increasing adoption on natural language processing (NLP) technologies in user-facing products including machine translation (Vaswani et al., 2017; Lewis et al., 2020), dialogue systems (Andreas et al., 2020; Gangadharaiah and Narayanaswamy, 2020) and recommendation systems (Jannach et al., 2020) the NLP community is becoming increasingly aware that we have a responsibility to evaluate the effects of our research and mitigate harmful outcomes (Bender et al., 2021). Indeed, models have been shown to introduce vulnerabilities and threats, both inadvertent and malicious, to individual users, social groups, and content integrity. Without social context and content control, deployed language generators have quickly derailed to racist, homophobic, hateful comments (Hunt, 2016; Jang, 2021; Wolf et al., 2017; Vincent, 2022), compromised user privacy (Carlini et al., 2021), spread disinformation (Shao et al., 2018), and even encouraged suicide (Daws, 2020). Prior works have outlined these risks (Maynez et al., 2020; Sheng et al., 2021; Weidinger et al., 2021), proposed taxonomies (Weidinger et al., 2022), discussed their points of origin, and advocated for research on ethical development of LMs (Bender et al., 2021; Solaiman et al., 2019).

However, there is little work that summarizes **actionable approaches and technical solutions** to preventing or mitigating these harms. This is the purpose of our tutorial, which is based on a survey we have recently conducted (Kumar et al., 2022). In this tutorial, we aim to provide a **comprehensive, unified taxonomy** of relevant **mitigation strategies** proposed in prior literature, specifically focusing on **language generation models**.

2 Tutorial Content and Relevance

What are language models? A brief background: To build a common ground for discussing the risk mitigation strategies, this tutorial will begin with a brief overview of recent trends in language modeling and pretraining. We will cover both causal (Radford et al., 2019; Brown et al., 2020) and non-causal language models (Devlin et al., 2019) highlighting their differences and their impact on NLP research. We will briefly discuss how pretrained models can be adapted to different tasks covering model finetuning (both complete and adapter based) as well as prompt-based formulation to solve NLP tasks. We will also focus on their scale both in terms of model parameters as well as training data size.

How can language models cause societal harm? After presenting the background on language models, we will then give a formal definition of harms based on taxonomy defined in prior work (Barocas et al., 2017) and focus on *representational harms*

Proceedings of the 2023 Conference on Empirical Methods in Natural Language Processing: Tutorial Abstracts, pages 26–33
December 6-10, 2023 ©2023 Association for Computational Linguistics

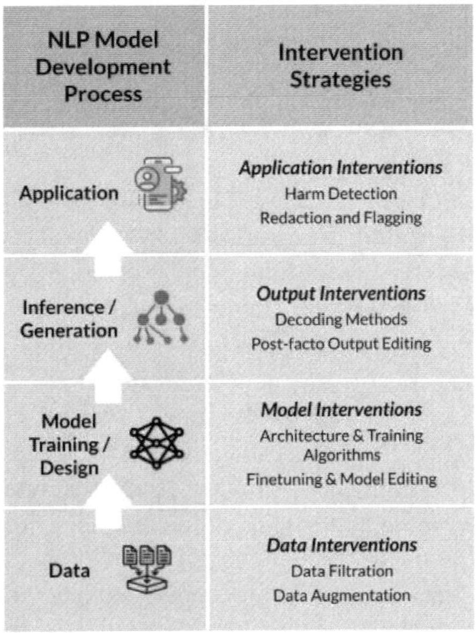

Figure 1: Overview of Intervention Strategies. Our survey presents a taxonomy of intervention strategies organized around the different phases where they can be applied.

in this tutorial. Highlighting the impact of heedlessly using web data which is usually population-imbalanced (Bender et al., 2021) and contains biased language against towards specific populations, we will discuss how language models tend to reinforce and amplify bias against sub-populations based on different personal and social attributes such as gender (Stanovsky et al., 2019; de Vassimon Manela et al., 2021), race (Liang et al., 2021; Field et al., 2021), region (Huang et al., 2020), demographics (Huang et al., 2020), age (Nangia et al., 2020) among others. We will also discuss, that by not being grounded in real world knowledge, they pickup on spurious statistical correlations in data and generate (in other words, hallucinate) factually incorrect content which can potentially be used to spread misinformation (Zellers et al., 2020; Kryscinski et al., 2020). Major content of this section is borrowed from the course on Ethics in NLP developed at Carnegie Mellon University and the University the Washington by organizer Yulia Tsvetkov.

Can we reduce or mitigate such harms? Finally, in this part, we will focus on work on mitigating harmful effects of language generation systems. While still a nascent field of research, several solutions in this space have been proposed which we categorize into four categories, visualized in Fig. 1. We organize and discuss in detail intervention strategies based on where they fit in different stages of LM development: **in data collection, modeling, post-factum decoding, and application**. Within each of these categories, our taxonomy brings together prior works that have been treated as disjoint areas targeting different types of harms (toxic/biased language and misinformation).

Since LMs learn and amplify biases present in the training data, we will first discuss data level interventions which focus on either (1) filtering the pretraining corpora to create more balanced datasets (Jia et al., 2020), or (2) finetuning trained LMs on sanitized data (Gehman et al., 2020a). Second, we will review model level interventions where we consider approaches which modify either the architecture or training objectives to induce or remove desired biases (Nan et al., 2021; Cao and Wang, 2021). Third, we will present methods to modify model outputs post generation using decoding and editing methods to demote or remove harmful content (Yang and Klein, 2021; Kumar et al., 2021; Cao et al., 2020). These techniques are especially useful for cases where it is impossible to modify data or models or even decoding strategies such as in case of GPT3 (Brown et al., 2020) which are only available through an API. Finally, we will end with application level interventions where we show how methods to flag and redact harmful content allow applications to shield such content from reaching users (Vaidya et al., 2020; Sun et al., 2019).

Throughout the tutorial, we will highlight both detection and mitigation approaches, as well as their specific limitations and shortcomings. By the end of the tutorial, participants will be better informed where to focus future research efforts.

Due to the vast range of societal harms and their mitigation strategies, we do not plan an exhaustive treatment of this material. One central goal is to raise awareness for participants of the relevant issues, so that when they return to their research they will be more able to notice ways in which their research based on large language models might impact different variety of users. To achieve this goal, we will aim for a "T-shape" in terms of breadth and depth: to briefly mention a number of core questions and then to drill down into a few particular case studies to see how these issues play out in real research settings.

3 Tutorial Structure

We propose a **cutting-edge tutorial** on an emerging area that has not been previously covered in ACL/EMNLP/NAACL/COLING tutorials. This would be a discussion-style tutorial where the organizers will present material with structured time throughout for questions, and discussion amongst attendees. The duration of the tutorial will be 3 hours with 5 min breaks at the end of each hour. The following would be the outline of the talk:

1. Brief Introduction to Language models (10 mins) - We will provide a quick background on current state of NLP research with introduction to language models and their capabilities.

2. Possible Harms of Language Technologies (15 mins) - We will briefly cover examples of ethical concerns, societal harms and biases present in current NLP tools.

- Fairness/Bias - Research on human-like biases in NLP (Field et al., 2021; Caliskan et al., 2017; Field and Tsvetkov, 2020)
- Toxicity - Research on toxic text generated by NLP models (Gehman et al., 2020a) and biases propagated in efforts to correct them (Davidson et al., 2017).
- Misinformation, Factual Inconsistencies - factual errors in generated text (Cao et al., 2018; Buchanan et al., 2021; Zellers et al., 2020)
- Privacy - Models generating sensitive, identifying information like addresses, SSN, etc. (Carlini et al., 2020; Inan et al., 2021)

3. Application Level Interventions (30 mins) - Techniques to filter harmful content before presenting model outputs to users.

- Harm Detection - Research on Toxic text detection (Vaidya et al., 2020; Han and Tsvetkov, 2020), fact-checking (Zhou et al., 2021), hallucination detection (Kryscinski et al., 2020; Goyal and Durrett, 2020), bias-detection (Sun et al., 2019; Park et al., 2018).
- Redacting or Flagging Harmful Text - Research on application level warnings or redaction for harmful or inappropriate generated text (Xu et al., 2020).

4. Output Level Interventions (30 mins) - Techniques to modify outputs to remove harmful content.

- Decoding Techniques - Research on search and sampling algorithms for controllable generation by promoting or demoting specific properties in output text (Zhang et al., 2022; Krishna et al., 2022; King et al., 2022).
- Post-Factum Editing - Research to edit or revise generated text to remove harmful content (Pryzant et al., 2020; He et al., 2021; Balachandran et al., 2022).

5. Model Level Interventions (30 mins) - Techniques to modify or optimize model parameters to prevent risky generations.

- Architecture and Training - Research on objectives and model architectures to enforce safe and reliable text generation (Yu et al., 2022; Nan et al., 2021; Falke et al., 2019).
- Finetuning and Model Editing - Research on editing or finetuning model parameters to incorporate safety constraints, through with new objectives (Gururangan et al., 2020; Chan et al., 2021; Gehman et al., 2020b; Chronopoulou et al., 2020).

6. Data Level Interventions (30 mins) - Techniques to curate clean training data to prevent models from using harmful text.

- Data Filtration - Research on filtering/removing training data instances containing toxic or harmful content (Ngo et al., 2021; Brown et al., 2020).
- Data Augmentation - Research on adding safer examples to datasets to offset the effect of problematic data (Mathew et al., 2018; Dinan et al., 2020; Stafanovičs et al., 2020).

7. Open Problems and Future Research (20 mins)

The tutorial will be a series of presentations with a set of references to related research papers and external demos. The presentation will cover a wide array of research on the topics from across the field. We will share the slides with the participants in advance. We will additionally share an online repository of relevant research material and online links to available code and demos to help participants navigate and use relevant research for their work. No copyright issues are expected as we will use open-source material.

4 General Information

4.1 Organizers

Sachin Kumar is a sixth year PhD candidate at the Language Technologies Institute, School of Computer Science at CMU. Sachin's research tackles critical technical problems in core language generation with deep learning, such as open-vocabulary generation, detection and demotion of spurious confounders, and controllable generation.

Vidhisha Balachandran (she/her) is a fourth-year Ph.D. student at the Language Technologies Institute, School of Computer Science at CMU. Her current research focuses on building interpretable and reliable NLP models with a focus on summarization, factuality, and KB-based reasoning.
Lucille Njoo (she/her) is a second-year PhD student at the Paul G. Allen School of Computer Science and Engineering at the University of Washington. She works in the intersection of NLP, ethics, and computational social science, working on identifying societal harms in NLP models.
Antonios Anastasopoulos (he/him) is an Assistant Professor at the Department of Computer Science at George Mason University, USA. His research focuses on NLP for local and low-resource languages and varieties, cross-lingual learning and multilinguality, and cross-lingual fairness.
Yulia Tsvetkov (she/her) is an Assistant Professor at the Paul G. Allen School of Computer Science and Engineering at the University of Washington, USA. Her research focuses on computational ethics, multilingual NLP, and machine learning for NLP. She developed a course on Computational Ethics in NLP and is teaching it at both undergraduate and graduate levels since 2017, and she is a co-chair of the ACL Ethics Committee.

4.2 Audience and Pre-Requisites

We expect participants from a wide array of backgrounds, including researchers, engineers, and end users of NLP technologies. Based on prior iterations of the tutorial, we expect an audience size of 50-100. No prior experience with NLP/ML is required, but we believe that our tutorial will most benefit those who are currently using NLP or are intending to use NLP tools in the near future in their research/products. An optional list of papers is presented in our survey paper (Kumar et al., 2022).

4.3 Diversity

The content of this tutorial highlights the impact of LMs on diverse users and therefore we aim to reach wide and diverse audiences. We will advertise this tutorial to diverse groups of researchers (e.g., Masakane, LatinX, North Africans, disabled in AI, indigenous in AI, Khipu) to bring in participants from various backgrounds. A previous version of this tutorial attracted audience from diverse gender, race as well as professional backgrounds like researchers, beginners and industry practitioners. Accordingly, our content will be made accessible to such audiences. Our own team is also diverse across multiple demographic attributes as well as professional expertise.

5 Logistics

Previous Editions This is the second iteration of the tutorial. The first edition of the tutorial was presented at The Web Conference 2022. While the previous iteration was focused to a general CS audience with less NLP background, this iteration will be modified to be aligned more for NLP-focused audience. This would entail including deeper technical specification of the interventions, including data, models and objectives.

Our tutorial is related and complementary to prior ACL tutorials related to bias and fairness in NLP (Socially Responsible NLP at NAACL 2018, Bias and Fairness in NLP at EMNLP 2019, Integrating Ethics into the NLP Curriculum at ACL 2020). Complementary to the content of the above tutorials which highlight social harms in NLP and discuss their detection, primarily focusing on representation learning and text classification, our tutorial will focus on practical methods to identify and mitigate harms in large language models and language generation.

Venue We prefer EMNLP or ACL, but any venue would work for us.

Technical Requirements We will not require additional equipment other than presentation material: an LCD projector, a computer with PowerPoint and Acrobat Reader, and internet connection.

Public Release We will publicly release all tutorial materials, including prerecorded lectures as backup for the tutorial which will be uploaded prior to the tutorial. These will be hosted on an open-access platform and linked from our University websites.

6 Ethics Statement

Although the aim of this tutorial is to improve the safety and inclusivity of NLP technologies and equip practitioners with tools to do so, we are well aware that as a not perfectly-diverse group of researchers we might incorporate our own biases into tutorial stricture and its technical focus. We will acknowledge this limitation in our tutorial, as well as the fact that the field of computational ethics is developing rapidly, and thus the content of our tutorial is inherently incomplete.

References

Jacob Andreas, John Bufe, David Burkett, Charles Chen, Josh Clausman, Jean Crawford, Kate Crim, Jordan DeLoach, Leah Dorner, Jason Eisner, Hao Fang, Alan Guo, David Hall, Kristin Hayes, Kellie Hill, Diana Ho, Wendy Iwaszuk, Smriti Jha, Dan Klein, Jayant Krishnamurthy, Theo Lanman, Percy Liang, Christopher H. Lin, Ilya Lintsbakh, Andy McGovern, Aleksandr Nisnevich, Adam Pauls, Dmitrij Petters, Brent Read, Dan Roth, Subhro Roy, Jesse Rusak, Beth Short, Div Slomin, Ben Snyder, Stephon Striplin, Yu Su, Zachary Tellman, Sam Thomson, Andrei Vorobev, Izabela Witoszko, Jason Wolfe, Abby Wray, Yuchen Zhang, and Alexander Zotov. 2020. Task-Oriented Dialogue as Dataflow Synthesis. *Transactions of the Association for Computational Linguistics*, 8:556–571.

Vidhisha Balachandran, Hannaneh Hajishirzi, William Cohen, and Yulia Tsvetkov. 2022. Correcting diverse factual errors in abstractive summarization via post-editing and language model infilling. In *Proceedings of the 2022 Conference on Empirical Methods in Natural Language Processing (EMNLP)*.

Solon Barocas, Kate Crawford, Aaron Shapiro, and Hanna Wallach. 2017. The problem with bias: From allocative to representational harms in machine learning. In *Proc. SIGCIS*.

Emily M. Bender, Timnit Gebru, Angelina McMillan-Major, and Shmargaret Shmitchell. 2021. On the dangers of stochastic parrots: Can language models be too big? In *Proceedings of the 2021 ACM Conference on Fairness, Accountability, and Transparency*, FAccT '21, page 610–623, New York, NY, USA. Association for Computing Machinery.

Tom Brown, Benjamin Mann, Nick Ryder, Melanie Subbiah, Jared D Kaplan, Prafulla Dhariwal, Arvind Neelakantan, Pranav Shyam, Girish Sastry, Amanda Askell, Sandhini Agarwal, Ariel Herbert-Voss, Gretchen Krueger, Tom Henighan, Rewon Child, Aditya Ramesh, Daniel Ziegler, Jeffrey Wu, Clemens Winter, Chris Hesse, Mark Chen, Eric Sigler, Mateusz Litwin, Scott Gray, Benjamin Chess, Jack Clark, Christopher Berner, Sam McCandlish, Alec Radford, Ilya Sutskever, and Dario Amodei. 2020. Language models are few-shot learners. In *Advances in Neural Information Processing Systems*, volume 33, pages 1877–1901. Curran Associates, Inc.

Ben Buchanan, Andrew Lohn, Micah Musser, and Katerina Sedova. 2021. Truth, lies, and automation.

Aylin Caliskan, Joanna J Bryson, and Arvind Narayanan. 2017. Semantics derived automatically from language corpora contain human-like biases. *Science*, 356(6334):183–186.

Meng Cao, Yue Dong, Jiapeng Wu, and Jackie Chi Kit Cheung. 2020. Factual error correction for abstractive summarization models. In *Proceedings of the 2020 Conference on Empirical Methods in Natural Language Processing (EMNLP)*, pages 6251–6258, Online. Association for Computational Linguistics.

Shuyang Cao and Lu Wang. 2021. Cliff: Contrastive learning for improving faithfulness and factuality in abstractive summarization.

Ziqiang Cao, Furu Wei, Wenjie Li, and Sujian Li. 2018. Faithful to the original: Fact aware neural abstractive summarization. In *Proceedings of the Thirty-Second AAAI Conference on Artificial Intelligence, (AAAI-18), the 30th innovative Applications of Artificial Intelligence (IAAI-18), and the 8th AAAI Symposium on Educational Advances in Artificial Intelligence (EAAI-18), New Orleans, Louisiana, USA, February 2-7, 2018*, pages 4784–4791. AAAI Press.

Nicholas Carlini, Florian Tramer, Eric Wallace, Matthew Jagielski, Ariel Herbert-Voss, Katherine Lee, Adam Roberts, Tom Brown, Dawn Song, Ulfar Erlingsson, et al. 2020. Extracting training data from large language models. *arXiv preprint arXiv:2012.07805*.

Nicholas Carlini, Florian Tramer, Eric Wallace, Matthew Jagielski, Ariel Herbert-Voss, Katherine Lee, Adam Roberts, Tom Brown, Dawn Song, Ulfar Erlingsson, et al. 2021. Extracting training data from large language models. In *30th USENIX Security Symposium (USENIX Security 21)*, pages 2633–2650.

Alvin Chan, Yew-Soon Ong, Bill Pung, Aston Zhang, and Jie Fu. 2021. Cocon: A self-supervised approach for controlled text generation. In *Proc. ICLR*.

Alexandra Chronopoulou, Dario Stojanovski, and Alexander Fraser. 2020. Reusing a Pretrained Language Model on Languages with Limited Corpora for Unsupervised NMT. In *Proceedings of the 2020 Conference on Empirical Methods in Natural Language Processing (EMNLP)*, pages 2703–2711, Online. Association for Computational Linguistics.

Thomas Davidson, Dana Warmsley, Michael Macy, and Ingmar Weber. 2017. Automated hate speech detection and the problem of offensive language. In *Proceedings of the International AAAI Conference on Web and Social Media*, volume 11.

Ryan Daws. 2020. Medical chatbot using OpenAI's GPT-3 told a fake patient to kill themselves.

Daniel de Vassimon Manela, David Errington, Thomas Fisher, Boris van Breugel, and Pasquale Minervini. 2021. Stereotype and skew: Quantifying gender bias in pre-trained and fine-tuned language models. In *Proceedings of the 16th Conference of the European Chapter of the Association for Computational Linguistics: Main Volume*, pages 2232–2242, Online. Association for Computational Linguistics.

Jacob Devlin, Ming-Wei Chang, Kenton Lee, and Kristina Toutanova. 2019. BERT: Pre-training of deep bidirectional transformers for language understanding. In *Proceedings of the 2019 Conference of the North American Chapter of the Association for Computational Linguistics: Human Language Technologies, Volume 1 (Long and Short Papers)*, pages 4171–4186, Minneapolis, Minnesota. Association for Computational Linguistics.

Emily Dinan, Angela Fan, Adina Williams, Jack Urbanek, Douwe Kiela, and Jason Weston. 2020. Queens are powerful too: Mitigating gender bias in dialogue generation. In *Proceedings of the 2020 Conference on Empirical Methods in Natural Language Processing (EMNLP)*, pages 8173–8188, Online. Association for Computational Linguistics.

Tobias Falke, Leonardo F. R. Ribeiro, Prasetya Ajie Utama, Ido Dagan, and Iryna Gurevych. 2019. Ranking generated summaries by correctness: An interesting but challenging application for natural language inference. In *ACL (1)*, pages 2214–2220.

Anjalie Field, Su Lin Blodgett, Zeerak Waseem, and Yulia Tsvetkov. 2021. A survey of race, racism, and anti-racism in nlp. *arXiv preprint arXiv:2106.11410*.

Anjalie Field and Yulia Tsvetkov. 2020. Unsupervised discovery of implicit gender bias. *arXiv preprint arXiv:2004.08361*.

Rashmi Gangadharaiah and Balakrishnan Narayanaswamy. 2020. Recursive template-based frame generation for task oriented dialog. In *Proceedings of the 58th Annual Meeting of the Association for Computational Linguistics*, pages 2059–2064, Online. Association for Computational Linguistics.

Samuel Gehman, Suchin Gururangan, Maarten Sap, Yejin Choi, and Noah A Smith. 2020a. Realtoxicityprompts: Evaluating neural toxic degeneration in language models. *EMNLP*.

Samuel Gehman, Suchin Gururangan, Maarten Sap, Yejin Choi, and Noah A. Smith. 2020b. RealToxicityPrompts: Evaluating neural toxic degeneration in language models. In *Findings of the Association for Computational Linguistics: EMNLP 2020*, pages 3356–3369, Online. Association for Computational Linguistics.

Tanya Goyal and Greg Durrett. 2020. Evaluating factuality in generation with dependency-level entailment. In *EMNLP (Findings)*, pages 3592–3603.

Suchin Gururangan, Ana Marasović, Swabha Swayamdipta, Kyle Lo, Iz Beltagy, Doug Downey, and Noah A. Smith. 2020. Don't stop pretraining: Adapt language models to domains and tasks. In *Proceedings of the 58th Annual Meeting of the Association for Computational Linguistics*, pages 8342–8360, Online. Association for Computational Linguistics.

Xiaochuang Han and Yulia Tsvetkov. 2020. Fortifying toxic speech detectors against veiled toxicity. *arXiv preprint arXiv:2010.03154*.

Zexue He, Bodhisattwa Prasad Majumder, and Julian McAuley. 2021. Detect and perturb: Neutral rewriting of biased and sensitive text via gradient-based decoding. In *Findings of the Association for Computational Linguistics: EMNLP 2021*, pages 4173–4181, Punta Cana, Dominican Republic. Association for Computational Linguistics.

Po-Sen Huang, Huan Zhang, Ray Jiang, Robert Stanforth, Johannes Welbl, Jack Rae, Vishal Maini, Dani Yogatama, and Pushmeet Kohli. 2020. Reducing sentiment bias in language models via counterfactual evaluation. In *Findings of the Association for Computational Linguistics: EMNLP 2020*, pages 65–83, Online. Association for Computational Linguistics.

Elle Hunt. 2016. Tay, Microsoft's AI chatbot, gets a crash course in racism from Twitter.

Huseyin A Inan, Osman Ramadan, Lukas Wutschitz, Daniel Jones, Victor Rühle, James Withers, and Robert Sim. 2021. Training data leakage analysis in language models. *arXiv preprint arXiv:2101.05405*.

Heesoo Jang. 2021. A South Korean chatbot shows just how sloppy tech companies can be with user data.

Dietmar Jannach, Ahtsham Manzoor, Wanling Cai, and Li Chen. 2020. A survey on conversational recommender systems. *arXiv preprint arXiv:2004.00646*.

Shengyu Jia, Tao Meng, Jieyu Zhao, and Kai-Wei Chang. 2020. Mitigating gender bias amplification in distribution by posterior regularization. In *ACL (short)*.

Daniel King, Zejiang Shen, Nishant Subramani, Daniel S Weld, Iz Beltagy, and Doug Downey. 2022. Don't say what you don't know: Improving the consistency of abstractive summarization by constraining beam search. *arXiv preprint arXiv:2203.08436*.

Kalpesh Krishna, Ya yin Chang, John Wieting, and Mohit Iyyer. 2022. Rankgen: Improving text generation with large ranking models. *ArXiv*, abs/2205.09726.

Wojciech Kryscinski, Bryan McCann, Caiming Xiong, and Richard Socher. 2020. Evaluating the factual consistency of abstractive text summarization. In *Proceedings of the 2020 Conference on Empirical Methods in Natural Language Processing (EMNLP)*, pages 9332–9346, Online. Association for Computational Linguistics.

Sachin Kumar, Vidhisha Balachandran, Lucille Njoo, Antonios Anastasopoulos, and Yulia Tsvetkov. 2022. Language generation models can cause harm: So what can we do about it? an actionable survey. *arXiv preprint arXiv:2210.07700*.

Sachin Kumar, Eric Malmi, Aliaksei Severyn, and Yulia Tsvetkov. 2021. Controlled text generation as continuous optimization with multiple constraints. In *Proc. NeurIPS*.

Mike Lewis, Yinhan Liu, Naman Goyal, Marjan Ghazvininejad, Abdelrahman Mohamed, Omer Levy, Veselin Stoyanov, and Luke Zettlemoyer. 2020. BART: Denoising sequence-to-sequence pre-training for natural language generation, translation, and comprehension. In *Proceedings of the 58th Annual Meeting of the Association for Computational Linguistics*, pages 7871–7880, Online. Association for Computational Linguistics.

Paul Pu Liang, Chiyu Wu, Louis-Philippe Morency, and Ruslan Salakhutdinov. 2021. Towards understanding and mitigating social biases in language models. In *International Conference on Machine Learning*, pages 6565–6576. PMLR.

Binny Mathew, Punyajoy Saha, Hardik Tharad, Subham Rajgaria, Prajwal Singhania, Suman Kalyan Maity, Pawan Goyal, and Animesh Mukherje. 2018. Thou shalt not hate: Countering online hate speech.

Joshua Maynez, Shashi Narayan, Bernd Bohnet, and Ryan McDonald. 2020. On faithfulness and factuality in abstractive summarization. In *Proceedings of the 58th Annual Meeting of the Association for Computational Linguistics*, pages 1906–1919, Online. Association for Computational Linguistics.

Feng Nan, Cicero Nogueira dos Santos, Henghui Zhu, Patrick Ng, Kathleen McKeown, Ramesh Nallapati, Dejiao Zhang, Zhiguo Wang, Andrew O. Arnold, and Bing Xiang. 2021. Improving factual consistency of abstractive summarization via question answering. In *Proceedings of the 59th Annual Meeting of the Association for Computational Linguistics and the 11th International Joint Conference on Natural Language Processing (Volume 1: Long Papers)*, pages 6881–6894, Online. Association for Computational Linguistics.

Nikita Nangia, Clara Vania, Rasika Bhalerao, and Samuel R. Bowman. 2020. CrowS-pairs: A challenge dataset for measuring social biases in masked language models. In *Proceedings of the 2020 Conference on Empirical Methods in Natural Language Processing (EMNLP)*, pages 1953–1967, Online. Association for Computational Linguistics.

Helen Ngo, Cooper Raterink, João GM Araújo, Ivan Zhang, Carol Chen, Adrien Morisot, and Nicholas Frosst. 2021. Mitigating harm in language models with conditional-likelihood filtration. *arXiv preprint arXiv:2108.07790*.

Ji Ho Park, Jamin Shin, and Pascale Fung. 2018. Reducing gender bias in abusive language detection. *arXiv preprint arXiv:1808.07231*.

Reid Pryzant, Richard Diehl Martinez, Nathan Dass, Sadao Kurohashi, Dan Jurafsky, and Diyi Yang. 2020. Automatically neutralizing subjective bias in text. *Proceedings of the AAAI Conference on Artificial Intelligence*, 34(01):480–489.

Alec Radford, Jeff Wu, Rewon Child, David Luan, Dario Amodei, and Ilya Sutskever. 2019. Language models are unsupervised multitask learners.

Chengcheng Shao, Giovanni Luca Ciampaglia, Onur Varol, Kai-Cheng Yang, Alessandro Flammini, and Filippo Menczer. 2018. The spread of low-credibility content by social bots. *Nature communications*, 9(1):1–9.

Emily Sheng, Kai-Wei Chang, Prem Natarajan, and Nanyun Peng. 2021. Societal biases in language generation: Progress and challenges. In *Proceedings of the 59th Annual Meeting of the Association for Computational Linguistics and the 11th International Joint Conference on Natural Language Processing (Volume 1: Long Papers)*, pages 4275–4293, Online. Association for Computational Linguistics.

Irene Solaiman, Miles Brundage, Jack Clark, Amanda Askell, Ariel Herbert-Voss, Jeff Wu, Alec Radford, Gretchen Krueger, Jong Wook Kim, Sarah Kreps, et al. 2019. Release strategies and the social impacts of language models. *arXiv preprint arXiv:1908.09203*.

Artūrs Stafanovičs, Toms Bergmanis, and Mārcis Pinnis. 2020. Mitigating gender bias in machine translation with target gender annotations. In *Proceedings of the Fifth Conference on Machine Translation*, pages 629–638, Online. Association for Computational Linguistics.

Gabriel Stanovsky, Noah A. Smith, and Luke Zettlemoyer. 2019. Evaluating gender bias in machine translation. In *Proceedings of the 57th Annual Meeting of the Association for Computational Linguistics*, pages 1679–1684, Florence, Italy. Association for Computational Linguistics.

Tony Sun, Andrew Gaut, Shirlyn Tang, Yuxin Huang, Mai ElSherief, Jieyu Zhao, Diba Mirza, Elizabeth Belding, Kai-Wei Chang, and William Yang Wang. 2019. Mitigating gender bias in natural language processing: Literature review. In *Proceedings of the 57th Annual Meeting of the Association for Computational Linguistics*, pages 1630–1640, Florence, Italy. Association for Computational Linguistics.

Ameya Vaidya, Feng Mai, and Yue Ning. 2020. Empirical analysis of multi-task learning for reducing identity bias in toxic comment detection. In *Proceedings of the International AAAI Conference on Web and Social Media*, volume 14, pages 683–693.

Ashish Vaswani, Noam Shazeer, Niki Parmar, Jakob Uszkoreit, Llion Jones, Aidan N Gomez, Łukasz Kaiser, and Illia Polosukhin. 2017. Attention is all you need. In *Advances in neural information processing systems*, pages 5998–6008.

James Vincent. 2022. YouTuber trains AI bot on 4chan's pile o' bile with entirely predictable results.

Laura Weidinger, John Mellor, Maribeth Rauh, Conor Griffin, Jonathan Uesato, Po-Sen Huang, Myra Cheng, Mia Glaese, Borja Balle, Atoosa Kasirzadeh, Zac Kenton, Sasha Brown, Will Hawkins, Tom Stepleton, Courtney Biles, Abeba Birhane, Julia Haas, Laura Rimell, Lisa Anne Hendricks, William S. Isaac, Sean Legassick, Geoffrey Irving, and Iason Gabriel. 2021. Ethical and social risks of harm from language models.

Laura Weidinger, Jonathan Uesato, Maribeth Rauh, Conor Griffin, Po-Sen Huang, John Mellor, Amelia Glaese, Myra Cheng, Borja Balle, Atoosa Kasirzadeh, et al. 2022. Taxonomy of risks posed by language models.

Marty J Wolf, Keith W Miller, and Frances S Grodzinsky. 2017. Why we should have seen that coming: comments on Microsoft's Tay "experiment," and wider implications. *The ORBIT Journal*, 1(2):1–12.

Jing Xu, Da Ju, Margaret Li, Y-Lan Boureau, Jason Weston, and Emily Dinan. 2020. Recipes for safety in open-domain chatbots. *arXiv preprint arXiv:2010.07079*.

Kevin Yang and Dan Klein. 2021. FUDGE: Controlled text generation with future discriminators. In *Proc. NAACL*.

Wenhao Yu, Chenguang Zhu, Zaitang Li, Zhiting Hu, Qingyun Wang, Heng Ji, and Meng Jiang. 2022. A survey of knowledge-enhanced text generation. *ACM Comput. Surv.* Just Accepted.

Rowan Zellers, Ari Holtzman, Hannah Rashkin, Yonatan Bisk, Ali Farhadi, Franziska Roesner, and Yejin Choi. 2020. Defending against neural fake news. *Neurips*.

Hanqing Zhang, Haolin Song, Shaoyu Li, Ming Zhou, and Dawei Song. 2022. A survey of controllable text generation using transformer-based pre-trained language models.

Xuhui Zhou, Maarten Sap, Swabha Swayamdipta, Noah A Smith, and Yejin Choi. 2021. Challenges in automated debiasing for toxic language detection. *arXiv preprint arXiv:2102.00086*.

Creative Natural Language Generation

Tuhin Chakrabarty[1] **Vishakh Padmakumar**[2] **He He**[2] **Nanyun Peng**[3]
[1]Columbia University
[2]New York University
[3] University of California, Los Angeles
tuhin.chakr@cs.columbia.edu, vp1271@nyu.edu, hhe@cs.nyu.edu, vnpeng@ucla.edu

1 Introduction

Large language models such as GPT-3 (Brown et al., 2020), BART, (Lewis et al., 2019) etc., have advanced the state of the art in several natural nanguage generation tasks such as text summarization (Zhang et al., 2020) and machine translation (Liu et al., 2020). However when it comes to open-ended tasks with a focus on creativity such as generating stories (Fan et al., 2018a), poetry (Ghazvininejad et al., 2016), or various forms of figurative language (Chakrabarty et al., 2021), these state-of-the-art language models are often found to be inadequate.

The principal reason for this is that, in addition to composing grammatical and fluent sentences to articulate the intended content, these tasks usually also require extensive world and commonsense knowledge, as well as discourse modeling, to make sure the outputs maintain long-term coherence while remaining creative. It should also be noted that current approaches to text generation for specialized tasks require lots of training data for supervision. However, most existing corpora for creative forms of text are limited in size. Even if such a corpus existed for creative tasks, learning the distribution of existing data and sampling from it will unlikely lead to truly novel, creative output. Creative composition requires *deviating* from the norm, whereas standard generation approaches seek to mimic the norm.

This tutorial aims to bring awareness of the important and emerging research area of open-domain creative generation, with a focus on language generation while also touching on multi-modal generation (e.g., image captioning, visual metaphors, and visual story generation). It targets natural language processing (NLP) and artificial intelligence (AI) researchers as well as creative writing practitioners who are interested in building systems that are capable of emulating as well as augmenting human creativity.

In particular, we will review recent studies on creative language generation both at the sentence level as well as longer forms of text. We will provide the audiences with a holistic view of 1) the importance and challenges of building creative language generation systems; 2) methods for different forms of creative language generation such as story (Yang et al., 2022; Yao et al., 2019), poetry (Tian and Peng, 2022), humor (He et al., 2019; Mittal et al., 2022), metaphors (Chakrabarty et al., 2021; Stowe et al., 2021; Chakrabarty et al., 2020b), sarcasm (Chakrabarty et al., 2020a), and hyperbole (Tian et al., 2021) 3) how can models for creativity infer user intention and preferences, allow for fine-grained control, and take (natural language) feedback? In particular, how could the recent advancement of AI shape the future workforce for creativity? We will conclude the tutorial by outlining future research directions in this area.

2 Tutorial Outline

In this tutorial, we will review the history of creative language generation both in shorter and longer forms. Then, we will move to the recent advances in creative language generation that employ transformer-based language models as well as external world knowledge from existing resources. We will also touch upon how much creativity can we elicit from larger models like GPT3 (Brown et al., 2020) and where they are still lacking. Finally, we will discuss the real-world implications of creative language generation and how humans can interact or collaborate with these models to satisfy their specific needs. In particular, we will present recent community efforts in the following topics:

1. Reviewing the history of creative language generation and how neural methods have shown considerable improvements over prior

Proceedings of the 2023 Conference on Empirical Methods in Natural Language Processing: Tutorial Abstracts, pages 34–40
December 6-10, 2023 ©2023 Association for Computational Linguistics

approaches.

2. Introductions to contemporary methods for creative text generation along three main axes content planning for long-form creative text generation, figurative language generation with commonsense knowledge and the surprisal or twist factor which we term the XFactor in creative NLG

3. Discussion on how large-pretrained language models such as GPT-3 can perform creative language generation tasks and what are some of its benefits and where we can still have targeted improvements.

4. Introduction to the challenges in evaluating creative text. What are the possible dangers of relying on crowd workers from Amazon Mechanical Turk (Karpinska et al., 2021; Clark et al., 2021)? What are the tradeoffs of using expert vs crowd worker evaluation of creativity in language generation (Chakrabarty et al., 2023a)?

5. Examining how advances in creative NLG have opened up directions of research in the co-creative domain. How do amateur and skilled writers benefit from these models? How do these models fit into existing creative writing workflows? And how does this technology needs to improve to become more impactful and useful to end users?

6. Lessons learned open challenges, and discussion about how to build robust, reliable, and useful systems for creative language.

3 History

Due to the lack of vast research on creative language generation and its importance in training and testing generative models, it is necessary to have a cutting-edge tutorial on an emerging and timely topic. We are unaware of any tutorials on the exact same topic in the past 4 years' ACL/EMNLP/EACL/NAACL conferences, with the only exception of the ACL 2020 tutorial (Mou and Vechtomova, 2020) on Stylized Text Generation: Approaches and Applications. The tutorial was mainly about style transfer. While there are some overlaps between style transfer and creative language generation, we believe our tutorial will benefit the audiences in terms of learning the vast landscape of creative language generation in the age of pre-trained language models. Finally, our tutorial will also touch upon human-AI collaboration for creativity as well as creativity for vision and language tasks which has not been touched upon in prior tutorials.

4 Prerequisite Knowledge

Our target audience is general NLP conference attendances; therefore, no specific knowledge is assumed of the audience except basic machine learning and NLP background:

- Familiar with common natural language processing concepts (e.g., word representation, syntax, semantics) as found in an introductory NLP course.

- Familiar with the problems/setups of (open-domain) generation and creative forms of text such as story, poetry, metaphors etc

- Has basic knowledge about machine learning models such as deep neural networks, classifiers, and pre-trained models such as BERT (Devlin et al., 2019), DALLE (Ramesh et al., 2021, 2022), GPT2 (Radford et al., 2019), GPT3 (Brown et al., 2020) BART (Lewis et al., 2020).

5 Tutorial Content

This tutorial presents a systematic overview of the history and the frontier of creative language generation. We will also introduce methods for sentence level and longer forms of creative language generation, and careful consideration in designing the evaluation of model outputs as well as how LLM's can aid in providing assistance during the process of creative writing.We will then do deep dives. The detailed contents are outlined below.

5.1 Motivation, History, and Challenges [20 mins]

We will first motivate the importance of the problem by looking into works from psychology that examine what it means to be creative (Torrance, 1966) and then demonstrating practical applications of models that can produce creative outputs. Then, we will outline the challenges of building and evaluating creative generation models and systems. We will also include a brief introduction to the history of creative language generation and how many of the challenges encountered by the community when developing contemporary language models share parallels with those faced by researchers working on these problems prior to the advent of statistical and neural techniques in NLP.

5.2 Recent Methods for Creative Generation [75 mins]

We detail various contemporary methods for creative text generation along three main axes charting progress in each. [VP: This could use a bit more punch]

Content Planning - "Austen's Plots" [30 min] In this section, we will discuss how approaches to control the content of the generated text by sketching a plan (Yao et al., 2019) has enabled pre-trained language models to generate higher quality stories with coherent plot lines (Goldfarb-Tarrant et al., 2020; Rashkin et al., 2020) as well as poetry with form constraints like sonnets (Tian and Peng, 2022). We then discuss the recent phase shift to adapting this style of content planning to large language models such as GPT3 to generate even longer, yet coherent, stories (over 1000 words) via recursive prompting (Yang et al., 2022, 2023).

Figurative Language Generation with Commonsense Knowledge - "The Bard's Metaphors" [30 minutes] Pre-trained language models typically excel at understanding the literal meaning of the text and generating responses accordingly. However, when it comes to creative tasks, they often struggle to effectively employ figurative language, which is essential for adding depth and nuance to the text. We will discuss how incorporating commonsense knowledge from external sources (Bosselut et al., 2019) enables models to better generate similes and metaphors (Chakrabarty et al., 2020b; Stowe et al., 2021; Chakrabarty et al., 2021) and sarcasm (Chakrabarty et al., 2020a). Finally, we examine how chain-of-thought prompting can elicit better figurative language understanding that was learned during the pre-training of large language models resulting in opportunities to generate higher quality illustrations for the same (Chakrabarty et al., 2022b).

The X-factor - "Dickens' Twist" [15 minutes] Finally, there is the ineffable quality of creative writing which grips the reader to keep turning the page. While this element is most challenging to recreate from language models, we discuss works that attempt to do so by learning word-level relationships to generate puns (He et al., 2019) and break down intangible qualities such as humor into their basic principles for modeling (Tian et al., 2022).

5.3 Challenges in Evaluation of Creative NLG outputs [20 mins]

As the community makes progress in improving the various elements of the creative generation process, benchmarking progress becomes more challenging. One of the common practices in evaluating creative output is relying on crowd worker judgments from platforms such as Amazon Mechanical Turk. However, there are multiple challenges in these evaluations (Karpinska et al., 2021; Clark et al., 2021) such as crowd-workers spending limited time on reading and evaluating outputs, underspecified instructions for evaluation, variability in judgments across the same set of workers across different times, constructing proper qualification tests, setting up proper wages for crowd workers. A more promising alternative is to look into how experts might be better suited to evaluating outputs from creative NLG systems because their expectations might differ from amateur crowd workers (Clark and Smith, 2021). We discuss how recent work has delved back into the fundamentals of creativity to design evaluation axes based on the Torrance tests of creative thinking (Torrance, 1966) and measure these using expert judgments (Chakrabarty et al., 2023a).

5.4 Human AI Collaboration for Creativity [30 mins]

Recent developments in natural language generation (NLG) using large language models have brought us closer than ever to the goal of building AI-powered creative writing tools. In this section, we will discuss the potential of NLG to have a significant impact in the creative writing domain–especially with respect to brainstorming, generation of story details, and research assistance (Chakrabarty et al., 2023b). We will focus on different interaction interfaces for AI-assisted creativity, the extent to which they understand user intent, and finally, whether the human-AI collaboration improves the final creative output. We will end this section with the positives as well as limitations of current models as identified by expert and professional writers.

5.5 Conclusion, Future Directions, and Discussion [25 min]

We will conclude the tutorial by discussing future directions to build impactful, reliable and useful systems for creative language generation.

6 Tutorial Coverage and Suggested Reading List

While the tutorial will include our own work (Yao et al., 2019; He et al., 2019; Mittal et al., 2022; Goldfarb-Tarrant et al., 2020; Chakrabarty et al., 2020b, 2021; Akoury et al., 2020; Stowe et al., 2021; Tian et al., 2021; Tian and Peng, 2022; Padmakumar and He, 2022; Chakrabarty et al., 2022a; Yang et al., 2022), we anticipate that roughly 40% of the tutorial content will be pulled from work by other researchers in NLP and machine learning communities include but not limited to (Ghazvininejad et al., 2016; Fan et al., 2018b, 2019; Van de Cruys, 2020; Riedl and Young, 2010; Lin and Riedl, 2021; Brahman and Chaturvedi, 2020; Mirowski et al., 2023; Clark et al., 2021). A more comprehensive list of related papers will be provided before the tutorial.

7 Tutorial Instructors

Our instructors consist of experts who have conducted research in different aspects related to the tutorial topic.

Nanyun (Violet) Peng Nanyun (Violet) Peng is an Assistant Professor in the Department of Computer Science at the University of California Los Angeles. She received her Ph.D. in Computer Science from Johns Hopkins University. Her research focuses on the generalizability of NLP technologies, with applications to creative language generation, low-resource information extraction, and zero-shot cross-lingual transfer. Her works have won the Outstanding Paper Award at NAACL 2022, the Best Paper Award at AAAI 2022 Deep Learning on Graphs workshop, and have been featured an IJCAI 2022 early career spotlight. She has given a tutorial at NAACL 2018 on information extraction.

Tuhin Chakrabarty Tuhin Chakrabarty is a Ph.D. candidate in Computer Science at Columbia University and a part of the Natural Language Processing group, where he is advised by Smaranda Muresan. His research is supported by the Columbia Center of Artificial Intelligence & Technology (CAIT) and Amazon Science Ph.D. Fellowship. He was also a fellow at The New York Times R&D team working on Natural Language Generation. His overarching research question centers around how we can use large language models for creativity. He has published several papers in various NLP conferences and journals including ACL, NAACL, TACL and EMNLP.

He He He He is an Assistant Professor of Computer Science and the Center for Data Science at New York University. She is affiliated with the CILVR Lab, the Machine Learning for Language Group, and the Alignment Research Group. Her research focuses on building intelligent systems that can communicate with humans effectively and enable individuals to achieve their goals. Today's systems are often opaque, brittle, and difficult to control, which limits their usefulness in human-centered applications. To make them our trustworthy collaborators, her research aims to (i) understand the computational foundation of generalization in novel scenarios, and (ii) build interactive systems that align with users' goals. She has given a tutorial at EMNLP 2021 on robustness and adversarial examples in NLP.

Vishakh Padmakumar Vishakh Padmakumar is a Ph.D. student in Data Science at New York University advised by He He. His research is broadly in the field of natural language processing and human-AI collaboration with a focus on collaborative text generation for creative writing tasks and other interactive settings. Prior to this, he was a Graduate Research Associate at the NYU Center for Social Media and Politics working on political stance classification and multimodel content sharing in online disinformation campaigns. He has published papers at several NLP and machine learning venues including ACL, EMNLP, and ICML and was the chair of the ACL 2023 Student Research Workshop.

References

Nader Akoury, Shufan Wang, Josh Whiting, Stephen Hood, Nanyun Peng, and Mohit Iyyer. 2020. Storium: A dataset and evaluation platform for machine-in-the-loop story generation. *arXiv preprint arXiv:2010.01717*.

Antoine Bosselut, Hannah Rashkin, Maarten Sap, Chaitanya Malaviya, Asli Celikyilmaz, and Yejin Choi. 2019. COMET: Commonsense transformers for automatic knowledge graph construction. In *Proceedings of the 57th Annual Meeting of the Association for*

Computational Linguistics, pages 4762–4779, Florence, Italy. Association for Computational Linguistics.

Faeze Brahman and Snigdha Chaturvedi. 2020. Modeling protagonist emotions for emotion-aware storytelling. *arXiv preprint arXiv:2010.06822*.

Tom Brown, Benjamin Mann, Nick Ryder, Melanie Subbiah, Jared D Kaplan, Prafulla Dhariwal, Arvind Neelakantan, Pranav Shyam, Girish Sastry, Amanda Askell, et al. 2020. Language models are few-shot learners. *Advances in neural information processing systems*, 33:1877–1901.

Tuhin Chakrabarty, Debanjan Ghosh, Smaranda Muresan, and Nanyun Peng. 2020a. R^3: Reverse, retrieve, and rank for sarcasm generation with commonsense knowledge. In *Proceedings of the 58th Annual Meeting of the Association for Computational Linguistics*, pages 7976–7986, Online. Association for Computational Linguistics.

Tuhin Chakrabarty, Philippe Laban, Divyansh Agarwal, Smaranda Muresan, and Chien-Sheng Wu. 2023a. Art or artifice? large language models and the false promise of creativity. *arXiv preprint arXiv:2309.14556*.

Tuhin Chakrabarty, Smaranda Muresan, and Nanyun Peng. 2020b. Generating similes effortlessly like a pro: A style transfer approach for simile generation. In *Proceedings of the 2020 Conference on Empirical Methods in Natural Language Processing (EMNLP)*, pages 6455–6469, Online. Association for Computational Linguistics.

Tuhin Chakrabarty, Vishakh Padmakumar, Faeze Brahman, and Smaranda Muresan. 2023b. Creativity support in the age of large language models: An empirical study involving emerging writers.

Tuhin Chakrabarty, Vishakh Padmakumar, and He He. 2022a. Help me write a poem: Instruction tuning as a vehicle for collaborative poetry writing. *arXiv preprint arXiv:2210.13669*.

Tuhin Chakrabarty, Arkady Saakyan, Olivia Winn, Artemis Panagopoulou, Yue Yang, Marianna Apidianaki, and Smaranda Muresan. 2022b. I spy a metaphor: Large language models and diffusion models co-create visual metaphors. Preprint under review.

Tuhin Chakrabarty, Xurui Zhang, Smaranda Muresan, and Nanyun Peng. 2021. MERMAID: Metaphor generation with symbolism and discriminative decoding. In *Proceedings of the 2021 Conference of the North American Chapter of the Association for Computational Linguistics: Human Language Technologies*, pages 4250–4261, Online. Association for Computational Linguistics.

Elizabeth Clark, Tal August, Sofia Serrano, Nikita Haduong, Suchin Gururangan, and Noah A Smith. 2021. All that's' human'is not gold: Evaluating human evaluation of generated text. *arXiv preprint arXiv:2107.00061*.

Elizabeth Clark and Noah A Smith. 2021. Choose your own adventure: Paired suggestions in collaborative writing for evaluating story generation models. In *Proceedings of the 2021 Conference of the North American Chapter of the Association for Computational Linguistics: Human Language Technologies*, pages 3566–3575.

Jacob Devlin, Ming-Wei Chang, Kenton Lee, and Kristina Toutanova. 2019. BERT: Pre-training of deep bidirectional transformers for language understanding. In *Proceedings of the 2019 Conference of the North American Chapter of the Association for Computational Linguistics: Human Language Technologies, Volume 1 (Long and Short Papers)*, pages 4171–4186, Minneapolis, Minnesota. Association for Computational Linguistics.

Angela Fan, Mike Lewis, and Yann Dauphin. 2018a. Hierarchical neural story generation. In *Proceedings of the 56th Annual Meeting of the Association for Computational Linguistics (Volume 1: Long Papers)*, pages 889–898, Melbourne, Australia. Association for Computational Linguistics.

Angela Fan, Mike Lewis, and Yann Dauphin. 2018b. Hierarchical neural story generation. In *Proceedings of the 56th Annual Meeting of the Association for Computational Linguistics (Volume 1: Long Papers)*, pages 889–898.

Angela Fan, Mike Lewis, and Yann Dauphin. 2019. Strategies for structuring story generation. In *Proceedings of the 57th Annual Meeting of the Association for Computational Linguistics*, pages 2650–2660, Florence, Italy. Association for Computational Linguistics.

Marjan Ghazvininejad, Xing Shi, Yejin Choi, and Kevin Knight. 2016. Generating topical poetry. In *Proceedings of the 2016 Conference on Empirical Methods in Natural Language Processing*.

Seraphina Goldfarb-Tarrant, Tuhin Chakrabarty, Ralph Weischedel, and Nanyun Peng. 2020. Content planning for neural story generation with aristotelian rescoring. In *Proceedings of the 2020 Conference on Empirical Methods in Natural Language Processing (EMNLP)*, pages 4319–4338.

He He, Nanyun Peng, and Percy Liang. 2019. Pun generation with surprise. In *Proceedings of the 2019 Conference of the North American Chapter of the Association for Computational Linguistics: Human Language Technologies, Volume 1 (Long and Short Papers)*, pages 1734–1744, Minneapolis, Minnesota. Association for Computational Linguistics.

Marzena Karpinska, Nader Akoury, and Mohit Iyyer. 2021. The perils of using mechanical turk to evaluate open-ended text generation. In *Proceedings of the*

2021 Conference on Empirical Methods in Natural Language Processing, pages 1265–1285.

Mike Lewis, Yinhan Liu, Naman Goyal, Marjan Ghazvininejad, Abdelrahman Mohamed, Omer Levy, Ves Stoyanov, and Luke Zettlemoyer. 2019. Bart: Denoising sequence-to-sequence pre-training for natural language generation, translation, and comprehension. *arXiv preprint arXiv:1910.13461*.

Mike Lewis, Yinhan Liu, Naman Goyal, Marjan Ghazvininejad, Abdelrahman Mohamed, Omer Levy, Veselin Stoyanov, and Luke Zettlemoyer. 2020. BART: Denoising sequence-to-sequence pre-training for natural language generation, translation, and comprehension. In *Proceedings of the 58th Annual Meeting of the Association for Computational Linguistics*, pages 7871–7880, Online. Association for Computational Linguistics.

Zhiyu Lin and Mark O. Riedl. 2021. Plug-and-blend: A framework for controllable story generation with blended control codes. In *Proceedings of the 2021 AAAI Conference on AI and Interactive Digital Entertainment*.

Yinhan Liu, Jiatao Gu, Naman Goyal, Xian Li, Sergey Edunov, Marjan Ghazvininejad, Mike Lewis, and Luke Zettlemoyer. 2020. Multilingual denoising pre-training for neural machine translation. *Transactions of the Association for Computational Linguistics*, 8:726–742.

Piotr Mirowski, Kory W. Mathewson, Jaylen Pittman, and Richard Evans. 2023. Co-writing screenplays and theatre scripts with language models: Evaluation by industry professionals. In *Proceedings of the 2023 CHI Conference on Human Factors in Computing Systems*, CHI '23, New York, NY, USA. Association for Computing Machinery.

Anirudh Mittal, Yufei Tian, and Nanyun Peng. 2022. AmbiPun: Generating humorous puns with ambiguous context. In *Proceedings of the 2022 Conference of the North American Chapter of the Association for Computational Linguistics: Human Language Technologies*, pages 1053–1062, Seattle, United States. Association for Computational Linguistics.

Lili Mou and Olga Vechtomova. 2020. Stylized text generation: Approaches and applications. In *Proceedings of the 58th Annual Meeting of the Association for Computational Linguistics: Tutorial Abstracts*, pages 19–22, Online. Association for Computational Linguistics.

Vishakh Padmakumar and He He. 2022. Machine-in-the-loop rewriting for creative image captioning. In *Proceedings of the 2022 Conference of the North American Chapter of the Association for Computational Linguistics: Human Language Technologies*, pages 573–586, Seattle, United States. Association for Computational Linguistics.

Alec Radford, Jeff Wu, Rewon Child, David Luan, Dario Amodei, and Ilya Sutskever. 2019. Language models are unsupervised multitask learners.

Aditya Ramesh, Prafulla Dhariwal, Alex Nichol, Casey Chu, and Mark Chen. 2022. Hierarchical text-conditional image generation with clip latents. *arXiv preprint arXiv:2204.06125*.

Aditya Ramesh, Mikhail Pavlov, Gabriel Goh, Scott Gray, Chelsea Voss, Alec Radford, Mark Chen, and Ilya Sutskever. 2021. Zero-shot text-to-image generation. In *International Conference on Machine Learning*, pages 8821–8831. PMLR.

Hannah Rashkin, Asli Celikyilmaz, Yejin Choi, and Jianfeng Gao. 2020. PlotMachines: Outline-conditioned generation with dynamic plot state tracking. In *Proceedings of the 2020 Conference on Empirical Methods in Natural Language Processing (EMNLP)*, pages 4274–4295, Online. Association for Computational Linguistics.

Mark O Riedl and Robert Michael Young. 2010. Narrative planning: Balancing plot and character. *Journal of Artificial Intelligence Research*, 39:217–268.

Kevin Stowe, Tuhin Chakrabarty, Nanyun Peng, Smaranda Muresan, and Iryna Gurevych. 2021. Metaphor generation with conceptual mappings. In *Proceedings of the 59th Annual Meeting of the Association for Computational Linguistics and the 11th International Joint Conference on Natural Language Processing (Volume 1: Long Papers)*, pages 6724–6736, Online. Association for Computational Linguistics.

Yufei Tian and Nanyun Peng. 2022. Zero-shot sonnet generation with discourse-level planning and aesthetics features. In *Proceedings of the 2022 Conference of the North American Chapter of the Association for Computational Linguistics: Human Language Technologies*, pages 3587–3597, Seattle, United States. Association for Computational Linguistics.

Yufei Tian, Divyanshu Sheth, and Nanyun Peng. 2022. A unified framework for pun generation with humor principles.

Yufei Tian, Arvind krishna Sridhar, and Nanyun Peng. 2021. HypoGen: Hyperbole generation with commonsense and counterfactual knowledge. In *Findings of the Association for Computational Linguistics: EMNLP 2021*, pages 1583–1593, Punta Cana, Dominican Republic. Association for Computational Linguistics.

E Paul Torrance. 1966. Torrance tests of creative thinking. *Educational and Psychological Measurement*.

Tim Van de Cruys. 2020. Automatic poetry generation from prosaic text. In *Proceedings of the 58th Annual Meeting of the Association for Computational Linguistics*, pages 2471–2480, Online. Association for Computational Linguistics.

Kevin Yang, Dan Klein, Nanyun Peng, and Yuandong Tian. 2023. DOC: Improving long story coherence with detailed outline control. In *Proceedings of the 61st Annual Meeting of the Association for Computational Linguistics (Volume 1: Long Papers)*, pages 3378–3465, Toronto, Canada. Association for Computational Linguistics.

Kevin Yang, Yuandong Tian, Nanyun Peng, and Dan Klein. 2022. Re3: Generating longer stories with recursive reprompting and revision. In *Proceedings of the 2022 Conference on Empirical Methods in Natural Language Processing (EMNLP)*.

Lili Yao, Nanyun Peng, Ralph Weischedel, Kevin Knight, Dongyan Zhao, and Rui Yan. 2019. Plan-and-write: Towards better automatic storytelling. In *Proceedings of the AAAI Conference on Artificial Intelligence*, volume 33, pages 7378–7385.

Jingqing Zhang, Yao Zhao, Mohammad Saleh, and Peter Liu. 2020. Pegasus: Pre-training with extracted gap-sentences for abstractive summarization. In *International Conference on Machine Learning*, pages 11328–11339. PMLR.

Author Index

Association for Computational Linguistics
209 N. Eighth Street
Stroudsburg, Pennsylvania 18360

ISBN 978-1-7138-8592-4

CURRAN ASSOCIATES INC.
proceedings.com

2nd Workshop on Deriving Insights From User-Generated Text (WIT 2022)

Dublin, Ireland
27 May 2022